Never Stop Walking

Never Stop Walking

A Memoir of Finding
Home Across the World

CHRISTINA RICKARDSSON

Translated by Tara F. Chace

Previously published as *Sluta aldrig gå - från gatan i* São *Paulo till Vindeln i Norrland*
by Bokförlaget Forum in Sweden in 2016. Translated from the Swedish by
Tara F. Chace. First published in English by AmazonCrossing in 2018.

Published by AmazonCrossing, Seattle

www.apub.com

Amazon, the Amazon logo, and AmazonCrossing are trademarks of Amazon.com,
Inc., or its affiliates.

ISBN-13: 9781503901612 (paperback)
ISBN-10: 1503901610 (paperback)
ISBN-13: 9781503900967 (hardcover)
ISBN-10: 1503900967 (hardcover)

Cover design by PEPE *nymi*

Cover photo used with permission of Helén Karlsson 2016

Printed in the United States of America

First edition

*I dedicate this book to the three women
in my life who made all the difference,
who gave me the light to find my way in the dark.
You gave me love to handle the hate.
You taught me to laugh so I could always find comfort.
You gave me sense when I didn't understand.
During our short time together,
you gave me enough love
to know what love really is.
This book is dedicated to you,
Petronilia Maria Coelho, Camile,
and Lili-ann Rickardsson.
Wherever you are, know that I am always with you.*

*This book is also dedicated to all the street children in
Brazil and around the world.
You are magical and deserve so much
more than society gives you.*

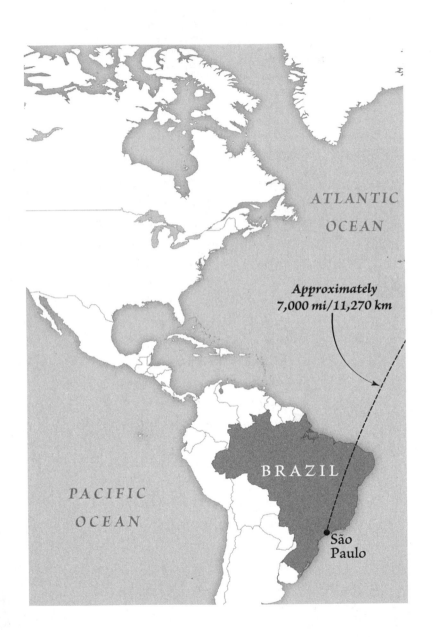

ATLANTIC
OCEAN

*Approximately
7,000 mi/11,270 km*

BRAZIL

PACIFIC
OCEAN

São
Paulo

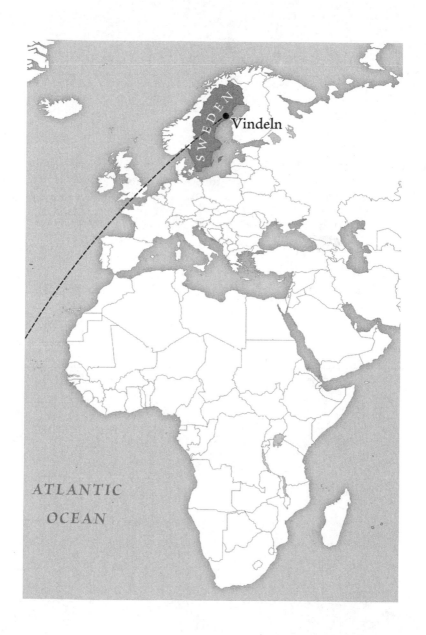

NEVER

from the streets of São Paulo, Brazil

STOP

to the village of Vindeln in northern Sweden

WALKING

Foreword

This is the story of my childhood in Brazil, about the culture shock I experienced when I arrived in the forests of northern Sweden and about the loss of the people I loved most. It's about what I remember of my childhood in the Brazilian wilderness, on the streets of São Paulo, in the orphanage. And it's about my early days in Sweden, when I found myself dropped into a place and life that couldn't have been in sharper contrast to what I had known. My memories are scattered, but the ones that remain are very clear. I have tended them carefully, repeated them to myself, and written them down to try to preserve the person I was. I created this story, my story. I don't remember exactly how old I was when each thing happened, or how long I stayed at each place. What is time to a child living in the streets? Why would we, I, need to know anything about time? We weren't part of society. We existed in a world that had no time for us, that didn't care whether we received an education, whether we lived or died.

Do you ever want to stand on a mountaintop, look out over the woods and the water, take in all the beauty at your feet, and then scream as loud as you can? Scream until you run out of breath, until your throat hurts and your lungs burn? A scream that cleanses the soul, a scream that lets you grieve and release the pressure of everything you've hidden away, all the pain you've amassed, all the adapting you've had to do. I have always adapted—to the laws of life on the streets, to the rules at the orphanage, and then to my new surroundings in Sweden. There are two *me*'s: Christina from Sweden and Christiana from Brazil. It hasn't always been easy to combine these two *me*'s. Several times I've stood on the top of that mountain, desperately trying to scream, to rid myself of some of my frustration and grief. I open my mouth to let it out, but no scream comes.

The pages you turn here are my scream, the words my amplifier. But most of all, the pages of this book are my truth, my story—of my struggle to survive, of the courage it took to return home to Brazil to look for my biological mother and to find joy in this life. And of the love of mothers, which stretches to infinity and then back again to warm my whole heart.

The Journey Begins
Umeå, Sweden, Winter 2015

One sunny day three years ago, I woke up afraid. Terrified is more apt. I was terrified of living. I'd hit the wall. Everyone knows about that wall. You can hit it at different speeds. You can run, jog, or trudge into it. The faster you're going, the more it's going to hurt when you hit it, and the greater your injuries will be. It's simple math, an equation that makes altogether too much sense. I had run straight into that wall at peak speed, as if I were running a four-hundred-meter race.

How did it happen? If you'd asked my colleagues—my bosses and friends at work—none of them would have been surprised. I gave 120 percent to whatever I was doing. The truth, though, was that my life was in chaos. I was having a tough time with my family, relationships, friends, and with myself. So, I tried to focus on what I could control. How to explain an I'm-afraid-to-live chaos? Afraid to authentically feel? Afraid it would hurt? Afraid the people I cared about would leave me or die? Afraid that if I stopped running, I'd collapse? Afraid of who I was?

I was so tired, so worn out. I couldn't think anymore, and didn't want to. Thinking just led to anguish. I wasn't up to being human. I experienced something I never had before. My body and my subconscious took over, as though my soul had decided it was its turn to take the reins. That was when the nightmares came: I was seven years old again and running for my life; I relived it over and over. If only I were dreaming about scary monsters under my bed. Unfortunately, the recurring images were real. I was dreaming about what had happened to me when I was little.

I realized that I couldn't continue to handle this on my own. I understood that I had two choices: to give up or get myself out of this state. I remember walking into my bathroom and standing in front of the mirror. I looked deep into my eyes. I looked inward. I watched my eyes fill with tears as I realized that the little girl who had run for her life had just kept on running. I needed to stop running and once and for all, for my own sake, process what had happened. I said it out loud: "I can't run away anymore. I don't want to run away anymore. *I don't want to live like this.*" And for the first time in my life, I asked for help. For real.

I'm sitting on my sofa in my apartment in Umeå. I go through all the paperwork I've received from my father about my brother's and my adoption. It was quite a bundle, and now it's spread across the coffee table. Half the documents are in Swedish and half in Portuguese. In all the twenty-four years these papers have been locked in my father's safe, I have never asked to look at them. I've never felt the need. There shouldn't be anything in these papers that tells me anything about myself that I don't already know, that tells me anything about my life in Brazil that I don't remember. I've never felt the need to find out who I am, where I come from, or why I was abandoned. I know who I am, where I come from; most of all, I know that I wasn't abandoned. *Kidnapping* might be too strong a word to use for how our adoption transpired, but sometimes that's what it felt like.

My brother Patrick, or Patrique José Coelho, which was his real name, the one our biological mother gave him, was too young when we came to Sweden to remember anything from our time before. In our

Swedish family, that time was rarely discussed. There were surely many reasons for this, but I know only my own. I do know, though, that my brother remembers only one thing from his time in Brazil: he slept in a cardboard box. I confirmed this for him, because I was the one who put him in a cardboard box to try to get him to go to sleep. What's so fascinating about memories is how certain ones are saved and others are not; some vanish for good, and some can come back. I've tried, but I can't remember my mother being pregnant with Patrick. It feels like something I would have remembered as a kid—my mother's tummy growing, and my knowing that I was going to have a brother or sister. I don't know whether I have no recollection because I spent most of my time on the streets without my mother, or whether I quite simply can't remember. I only know that one day Patrick, my little brother, was in my life, and that I loved him from the very first moment. I recall how I took care of him on the streets, how I fed him and changed his cloth diapers and made sure he slept sometimes. I remember that he wasn't a fussy baby, and he didn't seem to cry very much.

I was eight years old when I came to Sweden, and my brother was twenty-two months. We are half siblings. We have the same mother but different fathers. In the adoption papers, I can read who Patrick's father is, but in mine, the line for *father* is empty. I wonder if that means I'll never find out who my biological father is. It feels weird to say that Patrick and I are half siblings. Maybe that's because I didn't know my father or Patrick's. Because our fathers were absent, I've always viewed Patrick as my full brother. Maybe being adopted and getting a new mother and father also strengthened the bond between us as brother and sister. We became a family, a family defined not by blood, but by circumstances, by chance and, who knows, maybe by something inexplicable. But a family was what we became. Patrick was curious and asked questions: "Where do I come from?" and "Who are my biological parents, and why did they give me up?" I've never had those thoughts. I've wondered who my biological father is, but I've never felt that knowing his identity mattered. He was never there. That was normal for me. My brother and I have had different lives. Whereas he's basically only ever lived a Swedish life, I've lived both a Brazilian and a Swedish one. Which of us has had it harder or easier doesn't matter. We've each had our share of sorrow, pain, joy, and happiness, just in different ways.

Emotions aren't always easy to understand or deal with, and my rational mind isn't always enough to quiet the storm that sometimes rushes through me. Now is one of those times, as I sit here studying all this paperwork that tells the story of our adoption.

It's fascinating to read about what my adoptive parents had to go through to adopt and finally bring home the children they had fought so long for. They tried to have children for ten years but finally decided to adopt a child between the ages of one and three. In the end, they wound up with two children. There's so much paperwork: paperwork from the Swedish courts, the Swedish government agency that handles public health and social services, the court in São Paulo, and letters of recommendation from my Swedish mother Lili-ann's and father Sture's closest friends and colleagues. There's a letter that Mama wrote, and reading her words makes me both happy and sad. Happy that I can know some of her thoughts and feelings, but sad that she's no longer here with me. I wish she were, now that I'm about to start my search into the past. I'm a grown woman, an independent woman, but I doubt I'll ever outgrow the child inside me who misses her and needs her every day. Over the years, I've learned what it really means to miss someone. Missing someone doesn't have anything to do with how long it's been since you last saw each other, or the number of hours that have passed since you last spoke. It's about specific moments when you wish they were there by your side.

When I was a teenager, I asked Mama how she and Dad had reacted when they found out they were going to be allowed to adopt Patrick and me. Mama said they waited and waited for the letter that would confirm that they were going to get a child. When they were finally told they could adopt, they found out that instead of one child, they would be raising two. The girl was eight and her brother almost two. Mama said that when Dad found out, he disappeared into the woods for two days. Mama said that she told the adoption agency yes on the spot, though she was a little worried about how Sture felt. When he came back home to Mama and saw how worried she was about how he was going to respond, all he could do was say yes. Sture usually smiles a little when he says that if they'd offered Mama five children, she'd have taken them all. I like that, like that Mama would probably have welcomed a whole soccer team of children if she'd had to choose between that or none. Mama told me that she couldn't have lived with the thought of separating siblings. And if she and Sture had turned this offer down, she didn't know if they would have ever been offered a child again.

I read on through the paperwork and feel a stab in my heart. I've read something I wasn't prepared for at all.

There's a lot I don't remember, but I know it's not true that my biological mother abused us. People were awful to us, but I have no memory of my mother being awful to us. We were neglected, yes, that's true. By Swedish standards, all street children are neglected, even if they have good parents. But I respond most strongly to what it says farther down in the letter—that I had said that my mother was "nuts." I wish it weren't true, but I know that I did say that. I know that I said it because it was expected of me. I never thought my mother was different, but who knows, maybe she was. As a child, it's hard to know what's strange and what's not. What I know is that I loved and still love her—and it hurts to read these lines, because I know what we went through together. I wonder who wouldn't go nuts being forced to fight every single day on so many different levels to survive.

I set down the adoption papers and sort through a bunch of old receipts, airplane ticket stubs, and hotel bills that Mama saved from when she and Dad went to Brazil to come get me and my brother. I'm searching for clues that would lead me back to the orphanage, to my biological mother, and to the neighborhood I lived in. I translate one receipt after another: the receipt from the pharmacy where Mama and Dad bought formula for Patrick, the receipt for clothes they bought us, and restaurant receipts, but nothing leads me in the right direction. São Paulo is a big city with more than twenty-two million inhabitants in the metropolitan area and with numerous *favelas*, as the slums of Brazil are called. Finding out which favela we lived in seems impossible. Among all these receipts, I find a white sheet of paper that is a little crumpled and folded in half. I unfold it. In the left corner is a stamp from the court in São Paulo. I recognize Lili-ann's handwriting. She had quickly jotted down a few notes about me: *Christina doesn't want to live like that.*

Had I said that? It hits me that if they told Lili-ann and Sture, my adoptive parents, this, they might have told Petronilia, my biological mother, the same thing. I feel a crushing weight on my chest. After everything my biological mother and I went through together, after all the love she gave me, the authorities in Brazil might have told her that I'd chosen to leave her, when in truth I had had no say in the matter.

As I read this, I feel I need to try to find her. I want to restore my birth mother's name and tell our truth, as I remember it, as I remember our time together and the love we shared in what feels like a totally different world, another universe. Because there's a big difference between choosing not to take care of your children and living in a society that doesn't give its citizens resources so you *can* take care of them.

I call the Swedish court and request copies of all the documents from our adoption. The woman I talk to says she'll do what she can. Three days later, an envelope containing the copies falls through my mail slot with a little note that says *Good luck on your journey, Christina.*

Cave Girl

BRAZIL, 1980s

According to my Brazilian papers, I was born on April 30, 1983. That was also the thirty-seventh birthday of the king of Sweden, on the far side of the Atlantic from Diamantina, Brazil, where I took my first breaths. When I was little, Mamãe (the Portuguese word for mother) used to tell me that I was born in the woods, that my father was an Indian, so I was half-Indian. I don't know whether this is true. I don't know whether she embellished the story a bit, made it a little nicer than saying she didn't know who my father was, or that he didn't want anything to do with us. But I've always liked her version, and for many years I chose to believe it. A part of me still wants to believe it's true. What I know and remember is that I spent my first years in the woods and caves outside of Diamantina with my mother.

Even though I was so little when my mother and I lived in the woods, I have many memories of our time together there. I remember that we lived in two different caves. One was near a red dirt road and the other deeper in the woods. I remember how Mamãe used to sit and weave together twigs and palm fronds to cover the mouth of the cave or to use as a mat for us to sleep on. I used to sit next to her, watching her fingers as they worked with the palm fronds to create a wall. I thought Mamãe was so powerful, and I did what I could to learn from her.

We would hide our machete in a hole in the wall of the cave and put a rock in front of the hole to keep out venomous creatures. Neither Mamãe nor I wanted to be bitten by anything when we stuck in our hand to get out the machete, our most valuable possession. Without it, we would have been helpless. Mamãe used it as a weapon, and we used it to make our way through the dense vegetation of the forest. We also used it to open nutshells and cut down edible plants—it kept us alive.

I remember that I had an armadillo and a little monkey as pets. Maybe *pet* is the wrong word, because they weren't really tame and we didn't have a house. The armadillo was kept more or less against its will, and the monkey came and went. My relationship with the monkey was anything but reciprocal. It used me for food, and then it would throw pebbles, nuts, and anything you could think of at me. As soon as its hunger was satisfied, it would quickly disappear. Mamãe would say the monkey was like a man, which didn't make sense to me. A monkey was a monkey, and a man was a man. When I asked her about it, she laughed. Once, I fed both the monkey and the armadillo at the same time. The monkey took its fruit, didn't thank me, and disappeared again just as quickly as it had appeared. I could have sworn the armadillo gave the monkey a look, as if to say, *You lucky monkey, run while you can!* I gave the armadillo a look to tell it that kind of thing was not OK. I was about to pick it up, when it rolled into a hard, little ball.

Mamãe used to say we could always eat my armadillo if it became too disgruntled with its situation. When she saw my reaction, she would laugh and tell me she was just joking, but if I changed my mind, we could still stuff it in the pot. I didn't understand what was so funny and felt angry when Mamãe said things like that. I loved eating meat, but I hadn't really understood that I was eating animals. Later, when I understood what meat actually was, I refused to eat it in protest. My protest didn't last long, though, since we were poor and hunger always won.

But my armadillo wasn't there to be cooked. I used to feed it insects because I thought insects weren't animals. One time I got so mad at the armadillo that, barefoot, I kicked him after he had rolled up into a ball. I made that mistake only once; an armadillo's armor plating is as hard as stone, and it hurt like crazy.

Mamãe taught me which plants I could eat, which fruits and berries were poisonous, and how to make fire. She taught me which animals were dangerous and which were less dangerous. However, that didn't stop a curious kid from constantly getting into trouble. I remember picking berries off a big bush. The berries were yellow and almost as big as table tennis balls. I knew that Mamãe had said I absolutely couldn't eat them, but a hungry stomach took over my three-year-old mind. To her horror, Mamãe saw me stuff my mouth full and start chewing. She came running, screaming for me to spit the berries out at once. I chewed a little faster in an attempt to swallow before she reached me. I remember her grabbing my mouth, jamming her fingers in, and scooping out the chewed-up berries. It hurt, and I started crying. She screamed at me to spit, and I did. Something in her voice made me understand that she was scared. She picked me up in her arms, carried me to the cave, and washed my mouth out with water. As she started boiling water in our little makeshift fire pit, Mamãe asked me over and over if I had swallowed the berries. I shook my head, but I was starting to feel sicker and sicker. I remember Mamãe swearing while she mixed some dried green leaves into the water. She stirred and then poured the water into a brown canoe-shaped plant that we used as a cup. She ordered me to drink it all. It tasted bitter. She asked me how I was feeling. I just shook my head, and not long after, the stomach pains started. I remember being in agony all day and all night, and I drank Mamãe's medicine water the whole time. I never again ate berries that Mamãe said were poisonous.

I used to climb to the top of the little hill above our cave and sit, dangling my legs over the edge. From there, I looked out over the mountains, the woods, the dirt roads, the water, and the sky and thought it was beautiful. Where I sat, I could see all the big mountains that surrounded our cave; everywhere I looked was green. The sky could be such a light blue, and the water gushed down over the stones. The only sounds I heard came from the woods, from the crickets and the other animals that lived there. A few times, I heard the sound of a car driving on the red dirt road down below. I didn't hear any voices other than Mamãe's and mine. Sometimes I came alone, and sometimes Mamãe came, too, sitting next to me and dangling her legs over the edge of the cliff as she told me stories. It was usually warm, and there was no wind. Some days, there weren't any clouds; others, there were tons of big, fluffy, cotton-candy clouds in the sky.

Once, when we were sitting there talking, I looked at all the clouds and thought that one day I would sit on a fluffy white cloud with Mamãe. I imagined that we would sit there and look down at the woods, the water, and Brazil. I would hold Mamãe's hand, and we would bounce from cloud to cloud. I remember saying I wanted to sit on the clouds with her. And she said she didn't know whether that was possible, but she promised we would try. One day, Mamãe and I would fly.

Mamãe told stories about animals, angels, and God. I listened eagerly and had thousands of questions. Sometimes it felt like she wanted to scare me a little, like when she told me the story about the cow that was eaten by an anaconda.

There was a farmer whose farm was not far from our cave. One day, he was walking his cows down to the water to drink. After a pleasant afternoon siesta in the shade, the farmer woke up because the cows were running away in a panic, except for one lone cow that remained standing out in the water, not far from shore. It moved back and forth. The farmer walked closer and saw that a large anaconda was biting the cow's face. The farmer didn't dare go into the water to help the cow. All he could do was watch, hour after hour, as the snake tired out the cow until it couldn't struggle anymore and finally collapsed, exhausted. Then the enormous snake started coiling its body around the cow, and the farmer could hear the cow's bones being crushed as the snake constricted. Then it started swallowing the cow, head first.

Mamãe looked over at me when she finished telling the story and said that you never knew what was hiding in the water's depths.

I protested and said there was no way a snake could eat up a whole moo-cow, right? Because if it could, then it could eat me up, couldn't it? Mamãe said I was probably pretty tasty, and it would be a lucky snake who got to eat me. "But, Mamãe, if a snake eats me up, then won't I turn into poop?" I asked. Mamãe laughed and said that was exactly what I would turn into.

I remember that I didn't want to believe Mamãe's story about the cow and the snake, but her cautionary tale worked, and I was always extra careful when I went swimming—and I am to this day.

The time we spent together in the caves was mostly happy. Those memories haven't haunted me. The biggest things we had to contend with were finding food, hunger if we failed to find food, and surviving venomous snakes, spiders, and scorpions. I remember waking up in the middle of the night because a giant poisonous centipede was crawling up my thigh. I just swatted it away and went back to sleep next to my mother. I felt safe and warm. Whatever Mamãe did, I did. I spent my days playing with tadpoles and all the creatures I could find.

One day, I found a bird's nest in the cave with a chirping baby bird in it. Mamãe said the bird's mother wouldn't come back because it was afraid of us. I said we had to save the little bird; the feeling I had of wanting to protect and help it was unbelievably strong. I cared so much about that abandoned bird. It had an orange beak and pink skin peeking through downy black feathers. I named the bird Downy. Downy squeaked, and he opened and closed his beak. Mamãe said the bird was hungry, so I took a little rice from the old paint can Mamãe used for cooking. I tried feeding the sticky rice to the bird but without luck.

Mamãe gently took Downy from my hand, killed a beetle, mashed it up, and fed it to the baby bird. I remember how happy I felt when my little one ate. When I asked whether Downy would survive, my mother said that all she knew was that he would die sooner or later, but he was here now and all was well. When I asked if we would die, she said we would always have each other.

I didn't really believe that was the answer to my question, but all I cared about was us being together forever. I didn't know what death was, just that it had something to do with going away and not being visible anymore. Sometimes if I closed my eyes, I felt like I was the only one alive since I couldn't see anyone else. What I remember clearly is that I thought and felt that dying wasn't anything good.

Mamãe usually told me the truth, no matter how bad it was. Poor people like us couldn't afford not to know the truth. "Without it, we wouldn't survive," Mamãe used to say. We could dream ourselves away, dream of a nice house, warm beds, food and so forth, but we always had to keep dreams and reality separate. The reality was that we would never be rich and that we would always be considered "rats." The sooner you accepted it, the better your chance of survival.

When I think back on this as an adult, I realize that my mother usually told it like it was, but in the best and gentlest way she could. She chose to tell me the truth, and that has always made me feel loved. She saw me and took my ideas seriously. Who knows, the situation might have been different if we'd had money and a stable home with a father and all the material things that many people consider necessities. But our everyday lives were different, and at least, right then, it wasn't such a hardship that I had no home, only a cave. Don't get me wrong: things were incredibly difficult for us, and I don't believe anyone should grow up that way. We fought to survive, and those times we went to Diamantina and slept on the streets, we were very vulnerable. But the cave was my security. I played, and when I wasn't doing that, I was doing what I could to help Mamãe get food and money. I fetched water, made brooms out of twigs and palm fronds to sweep and clean with. I picked flowers and searched for food. I didn't know anything different. That was my everyday existence.

I remember how happy I was when Mamãe taught me to make a proper slingshot and how to aim to hit my prey. It took me quite a while to learn how, but ultimately, I got to be quite good at it. Once I managed to shoot down a small bright-yellow bird with a black pattern on its wings. When I picked it up off the ground, I felt bad. But that quickly passed when I saw how very proud my mother was. I remember how proud I felt then. We ate the bird for lunch. Mamãe grilled it over our little fire pit. Once Mamãe plucked all its feathers, the bird was half its original size. There wasn't much actual meat on its tiny body. We ate fruit and some berries and nuts with the grilled bird, and Mamãe joked that soon I'd be ready to hunt jaguar. When we finished eating and Mamãe had tidied up, we played Indians. Mamãe put some of the yellow feathers in my hair. It wasn't hard to get them to stay in; she just pushed them down into my curls.

I have carried with me my memory of the slingshot, the bird, and playing Indians as a sort of proof that it's important to be aware of your goals, strengths, and rewards. As an adult, every time I set out to tackle a difficult task that I feel unsure about, I think back to that.

One day, Mamãe and I had been in Diamantina and got a ride home in a pickup. The driver stopped and dropped us off, and we thanked him for the ride. We started walking up the little path we had worn, which, after a few miles, led to our cave. When we got there, some cows were standing outside the mouth of the cave. They didn't seem as surprised to see us as we were to see them. Two cows had found a couple of our big bags of rice. They'd chewed through the plastic and eaten half the contents. When Mamãe saw that, she started screaming. She picked up some big branches off the ground and started hitting the cows. I realized Mamãe was crying and screaming at the same time, so I picked up some sticks and went to help her. But she yelled at me to stay where I was so the cows wouldn't trample me. Once they were gone, she walked over to the rice sacks and sat down beside them and sobbed. I walked over to Mamãe and stroked her hair, the way she usually stroked mine when I was sad or sick. She hugged me and said not to worry, that I didn't need to be afraid. I was anything but afraid right then. I was sad, because I knew what a struggle it had been for us to save up the money for the rice and how important it was to our survival. I sat down next to Mamãe and saw that the ground was covered with little white grains of rice. Mamãe started gathering all the rice, and I helped her. I quickly realized that it was going to be nearly impossible to pick up the rice without getting a bunch of dirt with it. Mamãe said it was OK, that we could rinse it. We stuffed all the rice, along with the dirt and grime that we couldn't get off, back into the bags. Mamãe carried the sacks into the cave and hid them from any other uninvited guests we might have.

I have many recollections of how we walked up our little mountain and down the other side to a big creek to bathe and fetch water. Often when we got there, Mamãe would build a fire. She would fill the large paint can with water and put it over the fire. A big thick tree lay across the creek and served as a bridge. The tree, which had probably been there for a very long time, was overgrown with green moss and other little plants. While Mamãe heated the water, I would walk back and forth on that old tree, looking for something to play with. Suddenly, I spotted something moving. It was a weird little animal with two small claws on its front, several legs along the sides of its body, and a tail that curled over. I stood there for a bit, watching it. It moved cautiously and turned around to face me. I slowly leaned forward so as not to frighten it and started reaching for it, to pick up my new buddy. Then I heard Mamãe scream, "Christiana, noooo!" Hearing the fear in her voice, I froze. Mamãe came running, her flip-flop in her hand, and before I had time to do anything, Mamãe smacked my new friend. The front half of the animal was smashed, and its back legs and tail kept moving for a while. Its tail jabbed at the air until Mamãe gave it another whack. I was terrified. Mamãe exhaled, grabbed me, and hugged me tight. She told me the animal was a scorpion, that it was dangerous and stabbed its prey with its tail. It poisoned you, and you died. I decided I would never play with a scorpion again.

When the forest couldn't provide food for us, we hiked into Diamantina. Mamãe picked various plants, and I picked a certain kind of flower. The stems were long and green, round and smooth. At the very tip, the flower was like a bristle of little green sewing pins with compact white flowers at the ends. We were going to sell them in Diamantina. I don't know if they were good for anything. They certainly weren't the prettiest of the flowers in the forest, so I assume we picked them for some other reason. Maybe they were the only flowers that could survive the long hike into the city.

The walk felt like an endless march, mile after mile. It probably was only ten miles or so, but when you're little and your legs are short, it feels a lot longer. I was always tired when we finally got there. I didn't own any shoes, so my feet hurt and sometimes bled; my muscles were sore and stiff. I had learned that there was no point in complaining. To stop walking before we got there wasn't an option, because if I stopped, Mamãe just kept going. I remember on those first long treks into Diamantina—I couldn't have been more than three years old—I would cry, and my mother would usually carry me for a little while. But then she told me I had to learn to walk on my own. So, I didn't complain, I just kept up. To pass the time while we walked, Mamãe would tell stories. When I was at my most tired, she used to take my hand and pull me along a little so it would be easier for me to walk. When we finally reached Diamantina, there were places where we usually sat to sell what we'd picked. But we rarely managed to sell anything. We had to beg instead, asking passersby for money for food, but without much success. Some people pretended we didn't exist, others smiled and said hello, and a few gave us coins or a piece of bread or fruit.

One strong memory I have from Diamantina is of the bus station. Every now and then, Mamãe and I spent the night there. It was around that time that I first started to understand that we were poor and what that really meant. People would look at us funny. Some spit on us as we sat there begging, and for all the world, I couldn't understand what my mother or I had done wrong. We were nice people who hadn't done anything to anybody. We were just trying to scrounge a little money so we wouldn't starve to death. I didn't really understand what money was or why it was distributed so unevenly among people. I knew we needed money to get food, but I didn't really understand how people got money. Begging and selling flowers were clearly the worst ways to get money. I saw that other children had better clothes than I did, that they had toys, that they had so much that I didn't have. I saw that other women were doing better than my mother. I was starting to understand that maybe I wasn't as good as the other children. When I asked my mother if I was worse than the other children, she said I absolutely wasn't. She said I was good just the way I was.

When we managed to scrounge a small amount of money, Mamãe bought what we needed to get by for the next little while. Then we started the long trek home, back to what felt like security at the time. On a few occasions, we hitchhiked with someone who was going in that direction. Those few times when we got rides and I got to sit in the back of the pickup were unbelievably fun for me. The road was bumpy, and bouncing up and down on the hard truck bed in the back hurt my bottom, but it was the closest I came to riding a carousel. I loved it!

The strongest and most wonderful memory I have comes from that time. It's of the two of us running in the rain. Later, as an adult, I realized how much pain and sorrow the recollection of this one experience had offset. When everything in my life felt like a struggle, when I felt like life was meaningless or that maybe love wasn't something for me, I closed my eyes and pictured Mamãe and me running in the rain. I saw her smiling, her love for me shining, as if I were the center of the world. I don't recall where Mamãe got the umbrella. I'm sure I was with her when she found it. I wish I could remember why we were on that gravel road in that downpour. That kind of rain only happens in the tropics. The sky opens up, and in just a few seconds you're drenched. When it rained, Mamãe said that was God crying. I asked her why God was sad.

"Who said you only cry when you're sad? Maybe God is crying tears of joy."

I mulled that over a bit as we walked in the rain under that black umbrella, which wasn't doing its job of keeping us dry at all. But the rain was warm, so it didn't matter that the umbrella didn't work very well. Then I thought of something.

"Mamãe, how do you know God's crying and not peeing?"

She looked at me, a little taken aback, and then burst out laughing. She laughed so hard, she couldn't hold the umbrella up. At first, I felt a little foolish. Had I said something wrong? Mamãe looked at me, so amused.

"You're right. We don't know if God is peeing, but I would prefer to believe that God is sharing his tears. What do you think?"

I understood what she meant and, well, tears were nicer than pee. We both laughed.

"Come on!" she cried. She took my hand and held the umbrella out in front of our faces like a shield. "Come on! Let's run!"

Oh, how we ran! I ran as hard as I could, the umbrella continuing to fail to keep the rain off. I was happy. I looked at Mamãe and laughed. I remember feeling that I never wanted this moment to end. I ran until my lungs couldn't take any more and my legs ached. Then I ran a little more. I didn't care that I was running barefoot on a gravel road and that my feet were burning. I loved my mother—she was the best, and we were always going to be like this.

Another memory strongly imprinted on me is my last night in the forest, the end of our life in the caves. I must have been about five years old, and I was asleep in the cave that was a little deeper in the forest. I was alone. From time to time, I took care of myself while Mamãe was away. On this night, I'd fallen asleep by a little log fire that I had proudly made on my own. Mamãe had taught me how to light a fire in a pineapple-like cactus plant that burned for a long time and would provide heat and keep the animals away.

I woke up with Mamãe shaking me, and when I looked at her, she had her index finger in front of her lips, shushing me. I saw that the fire had been put out. Mamãe whispered that we had to run. I didn't ask why. I could tell from the stress in her voice that now was not the time to ask. Something dangerous was out there. Mamãe took my hand, and we started running. We ran out away from the cave and up the little mountain. We didn't take anything with us, not even our machete. I was wearing only shorts. It was dark, and I could hardly make out what was ahead of me. Mamãe kept a firm hold of my hand, and as we ran, I felt the branches and twigs scraping my skin. I tried to protect my face. I was barefoot and couldn't see where I was putting my feet. It hurt, but I didn't dare say anything. I just did my best to keep up. I still didn't know what was chasing us. Suddenly, Mamãe stopped, and I could hear how out of breath I was. I had scratches on my face, my stomach, my arms and legs, and they stung. I could feel that some of the wounds on my legs were bleeding. Then I heard men's voices farther below us in the forest. I turned around toward the sound and saw a gleam of light from a flashlight. Mamãe whispered that I should jump down into the hollow in front of us, and I did so immediately. I understood that the men were after us and that the situation was more dangerous than if they'd been wild animals. Mamãe sat down in the little hollow with me, took some dirt, and started to rub it onto my face, my hair, my arms, my belly, my legs. It stung, and I flinched but remained silent. Then she did the same to herself. She reached up and grabbed a pile of twigs and covered the hollow. It was pitch-black. Mamãe sat close against me. It was so crowded that we could hardly move. I heard the men's voices approaching and dogs barking. I wondered why we were being hunted. What had Mamãe done? My legs fell asleep, and I wanted to change the position I was in, but I didn't dare.

Mamãe was completely quiet. I heard the voices approaching, and the dogs. And then I felt something crawl over one of my arms and up my chest. I very slowly nudged my mamãe's side with my elbow and whispered, "Snake." I was scared but didn't dare move. I knew the snake would sense my fear, because Mamãe had told me that snakes and other animals could. But I was more afraid of the men than the snake. I knew Mamãe would never choose to keep sitting in this hollow if what was outside of it wasn't even more dangerous. The snake had now coiled halfway across my chest and was heading toward my mother. Suddenly I felt her move, and her hand pushed against my chest. She had grabbed the snake by the neck. The flashlights approached, and one of the dogs had sniffed its way up to the edge of our hollow. The dirt that Mamãe had rubbed on us couldn't mask our scent.

I felt Mamãe move again, and as the dog moved its nose to the edge of our hollow, she brought the snake's head to the dog's nose. I heard the dog howl—a sound I will never forget—and then the dog ran away, the men following it.

I remember thinking that the snake had saved us, and all of Mamãe's stories about patron saints and angels suddenly felt believable.

I don't know how long we remained there, terrified out of our wits in that hollow, but it was a long time. I think I was so exhausted, I blacked out, because after that incident, I don't remember anything else from our time in the forest. What I do remember is that we walked on the roads and moved from Diamantina down to São Paulo.

I was born to a wonderful woman and mother—Petronilia Maria Coelho. All I know about her comes from my childhood memories. I don't know her now. I don't know where she was born, who her parents were, or what her childhood was like. I don't know who her first love was, her favorite color, or what kind of food she likes best. I don't know what makes her laugh from her heart. I wish, more than anything else, that I knew her, this woman who gave me life, who loved me, who laughed and cried with me for eight years. She taught me to distinguish right from wrong and showed me the way through all the darkness that would follow me for so long. This woman gave me an inner strength and laid the foundation for everything good that exists in me. What more could a daughter ask for? I got more than many other people did: a mother's love. In many respects, I lucked out, and I'm grateful for that. And I know that someday if I can give my own children half of what my biological mother gave me, I will have been a good mother. I love her so much.

I wish that I could at least describe what she looked like, but I can't do that, either. I haven't seen her in twenty-four years. There was a time when I could close my eyes and picture her, but over the years, the little details have disappeared. When I close my eyes now and think of her, I don't see her anymore. When I look in the mirror, I can sometimes see part of her, but I can't really tell what it is about me that reminds me of her. However, I am positive that if she were standing here in front of me, I would know it was her. I can live with not remembering exactly what she looks like, because I've stowed away the most important thing of all inside me, in my memory, and that's our time together. I have saved the feelings that go with these memories in my heart.

What I can say with certainty about this exceptional woman, Petronilia, is that her everyday life was anything but easy. She had to endure physical and mental violence. I can say with certainty that her dreams never came true and that she never had a fair chance of making them come true. I can tell you that she had feelings. She laughed and cried like everyone else. I can also tell you that she loved her children. She did what was in her power to do to look after us, and I am her biggest admirer. We can't choose the family we're born into. Some of us are born to parents who love us more than anything, who try to protect us. Others are less fortunate, born to parents who abuse them, who hit them, and who maybe don't want them. I was fortunate to have Petronilia as my mother. She couldn't give me material things. She didn't have a house, and she wasn't always able to give me food every day. But she gave me the finest thing a person can give—she gave me love. She listened, and she gave me her time.

There are moments in life when it feels like you're in a movie, when it feels like you're living in another world, one that's magical and wonderful. My time in the caves is like that for me. Sure, it was also difficult. But at the time, I couldn't imagine how much worse life would get.

My Bag Is Packed
Umeå, Sweden, Spring 2015

My ticket is booked. I'm going back to São Paulo. I'm significantly older than the last time I was there, and I have no idea what awaits me. I'm grateful and happy that Rivia, a recent friend and a "Brazilian Swede" like me, is coming on the trip with me for support and as an interpreter. Rivia moved to Sweden from Brazil with her mother when she was eleven, and I feel a sense of solidarity with her. She is literally an Amazon woman. She comes from the state of Amazonas in northwestern Brazil and is exactly the person I need now, because I don't know what I've gotten myself into. We're going to fly from Stockholm to London, where we change planes for São Paulo. It's a long trip. I'm on the phone with Rivia, and we're discussing our reservations and the trip. She is working in Stockholm and confirms that her reservations are all set. She says she'll be back in Umeå a few days before we leave. We haven't known each other that long, but soon we're going to head out on an adventure together. Like me, she has no idea what she's gotten herself into.

I still don't know if I'll be able to find my birth mother, the caves, or the orphanage I lived in before I was adopted. I'm living on hope now with a hard-to-describe exhilaration that resembles fear.

I text a few friends and tell them that it's all set; I'm going back. My friends are like my family. Without them, I would never have been able to do this. I call Emma, and we decide we'll all get together before I go. We chat for a while and agree to create an email group for our whole circle of childhood friends so that we can communicate during my trip. Then I write to my little brother, Patrick. After that, I collapse on the sofa with the computer and the phone in front of me. It's quiet, and I try to let it sink in—in less than two weeks I'm going back to Brazil.

On Friday night, I meet my friends at Rex Bar and Grill in Umeå. A delightful sense of serenity and joy comes over me. I enjoy a good dinner with four wonderful people whom I've basically known since the first day I arrived in Sweden. The endorphins in my body rise, and a euphoria slowly but surely starts bubbling up in me.

We spend the first two hours talking about how things are going at work and catching up on everything that's happened since we were last together. We laugh, console one another, exchange tips and advice, and, most of all, support one another. Many people might take a night like this for granted or call it an everyday luxury, but I call it a life luxury. Whatever life throws at us, we have one another, and for me that has made all the difference. I interrupt the conversation and tell them that I love them.

They stop and look at me, a bit surprised.

"Oh, Kicki, that's the wine talking now," Lina tells me.

We all burst out laughing. I think back to my very first friend, Camile. What would it have been like if she were sitting with us? I miss her and send her a silent greeting before I return to the present moment.

The two weeks have passed now, and Rivia and I are leaving tomorrow. I glance at the enormous suitcase sitting on the round brown rug in my hallway. *This is crazy,* I tell myself. *Kicki, you packed enough for at least two months. You're only going to be gone for two weeks.* I take the clothes out of what feels more like a big trunk than a suitcase. I sort through all the dresses, shorts, tops, and shoes, but instead of taking items out, I somehow manage to add more. I realize that I'm overdoing it. I'm bringing three dresses to wear when I meet my mother for the first time in twenty-four years, if I manage to find her. One dress should be enough. Too many emotions are whirling inside me, too many *ifs*. And I have no control over what's going to happen. I convince myself that if we do find my mother, she's hardly going to care about my clothes. I know it's definitely not what I'm going to care about. But the dresses stay in the suitcase anyway, along with everything else.

I get out the big pink photo album that my childhood friend Maja has made as a present for me and my Brazilian family, if I have one. The photo album is magical; she pasted in a couple hundred pictures from our childhood and teenage years, of our group of girlfriends, of her family, and of her son, Harry, and my adorable goddaughter, Greta. I can't describe how much it means to me that she took the time to do this. Maja and I grew up on the same block. She was my very first friend in Sweden. Our friendship never ends and has only grown stronger as the years have gone by. I put the photo album in the suitcase and close the latch. I look at the suitcase again and shake my head. I go to bed. An early morning awaits me.

I've hardly slept a wink when it's time to get up. I take out a pen and paper and write a note to Anna-Karin, who's going to borrow my apartment while I'm away. I glance at the clock and see I have fifty minutes until the plane leaves. Had I lived anywhere other than Umeå, a small town in northern Sweden, I'd have been panicking now, but it only takes five minutes to get to our little airport from downtown, and as long as we're there half an hour before departure, it's fine. I call to double-check that Rivia is in the car and on her way to come pick me up. She isn't. At first I think, *Typical Brazilian, always late!* but then

I realize that we both misunderstood who was going to drive, and I laugh. A few minutes later, she's outside my apartment building. I lock my front door and lug my suitcase, which weighs way too much, down three flights of stairs. I'd like to go back to my apartment and dump out half of what's in it, but it's too late.

When I emerge from the building, Rivia is waiting in her trendy little white Volkswagen. She raises one eyebrow when she sees my suitcase and says she doesn't know if it will fit in her car. We open the trunk and realize that it really will be a tight fit. We move her bag and try to squeeze mine in. After a lot of back-and-forth, we're finally seated in the car on our way to the airport. Forty minutes later, we lift off, and it occurs to me that maybe I should have packed my parachute, too . . .

A World Without Shelter

São Paulo, Brazil, the late 1980s

Swedish friends and people attending talks I give often ask me how it happened that my mother chose to live in a cave with her child. Sometimes I give a long explanation, and sometimes I just respond with a question: "What's more dangerous than poisonous snakes and insects?" Sometimes people supply the answer on their own; sometimes I answer for them: "People."

I don't know what motivated my mother to live in a cave with me, but I can guess. The favelas and streets weren't better alternatives. One of the first memories I have of living and sleeping on the streets of São Paulo is the night my mother and I stayed up talking about life. I had asked her a thousand questions, and my mother patiently answered them all. I remember that I asked her why life was so hard sometimes. My mother's response was simple, and I remember she didn't even need to stop and think about her answer: "Christiana, there are worse things in life than living."

When I asked what she meant, she explained that if you could feel joy and pain, then you were alive, even though it might hurt and you could run out of steam and lose your faith. But going through life like a ghost, being alive but with a dead soul, like an empty husk, was worse.

I didn't really understand then, but it wasn't long before I did. Mamãe saw that I was still pondering her answer. She said, "We can always pray to God that these ghosts find a better world."

We were sitting on some cardboard, which we would later sleep on. We had laid it out in the corner of a tunnel. The long side of the tunnel was open, and there was a street just outside. I saw a yellow phone booth across the street—in Brazil, they are often umbrella-like domes mounted on a post. To me, it looked like an orange. I knew it was called a "phone," but I didn't really know what you did with it. Then I asked a series of questions: "Why do you call?" "How do you do it?" "Why don't you talk like we're doing now?" My mother answered each question patiently, even though she must have been completely exhausted.

"Mamãe, does God have a phone?"

"I don't think so, honey, but if God did, what would you want to talk to God about?"

"I would ask why some kids are white, some are brown, and some are black. I mean, there are so many other colors, so why not make green kids or red kids?"

"That's a really good question! You'll simply have to try calling God sometime." She smiled and gave me a kiss on the cheek. "Just so you know, little monkey, you got the nicest color."

"But Mamãe, I'm poop brown," I said.

"Ridiculous! You're chocolate brown, and chocolate is both sweet and good, just like you. Better watch out that I don't eat you up!" Then she pretended to eat me, and I laughed because it tickled. I squealed for her to stop, but she pretended to take bites from my arms, my legs, cheeks, and fingers. "Poop brown . . . You're nuts, you know . . . What do you say, should we try to call God?" she asked when she was done pretend-eating me.

"But does God have a phone?"

"I don't know, but I mean, it's worth a try, right?" She stood up, and then helped me up. We walked across the street, hand in hand. There weren't a lot of people around. We walked over to the phone, and she lifted me onto her hip. She picked up the receiver and held it out to me.

"Christiana, what do you think God's phone number is?"

"I don't know."

"Guess!"

"Mamãe, I don't know."

"But guess!"

"Hmm . . ." I said the first digits I could think of.

She dialed the number, and I heard the phone beep for each digit she dialed. When she was done, it was quiet for a bit, and then I heard a weird sound. She said I should talk.

"But, Mamãe, it sounds kind of weird!"

"But you can talk anyway. God might hear you."

I looked at her. It felt weird.

"God, why don't children come in green or red? Why are they white, brown, and black?" No one answered. Mamãe smiled, took the receiver from me, and hung it up. She set me down again and took my hand, and we started walking back across the street to where we were going to sleep.

"Mamãe, I don't think God has a phone."

"God might have heard you anyway."

"Will God answer me, then?"

"Who knows. Maybe God will visit you in your dreams and answer your questions."

"Can God do that?"

"God can do anything."

When we returned to our corner and our cardboard boxes, Mamãe lay down against the wall, and I crawled in in front of her so we were spooning. She held me and whispered good night. I fell asleep happy that night. The next day, I woke up because cars were driving by on the street outside the tunnel and people were walking past. Many walked by without looking at us. One man spit at us, and his spit landed pretty close to me. I looked at the man and stuck out my tongue at him. Mamãe glared at me and said, "Christiana, that is unacceptable!"

My mother did so many things that amaze me now. She thought it was important for me to behave properly. Once you're over thirty, as I am, a number of your childhood friends will have had children. Most of them have somewhere to live, a permanent and safe place where they don't need to be afraid of being assaulted. If you are a parent, you know a thousand times better than I do what it means to bring a child into this world and raise it. For the life of me, I can't understand how all these poor, homeless parents around the world succeed in doing so much and doing so right by their children, even in the meager and tragic conditions they find themselves. Despite all the poverty and depravation, my mother had the will and the gumption to give me love. Raising me was important to her, and not just making sure I survived but also seeing to it that I learned to be good. The women and men who take care of children under such conditions are heroes, and they prove that we humans can be truly wonderful.

My mother knew that we didn't need to sink as low as the man who had spit at us. She often reminded me that God saw everything. God saw those who were good and those who were less good, and no one could buy their way into heaven.

"Christiana, people need to be nice to get into heaven. Goodness has to come from the heart."

It's kind of a pity that I don't believe in the same heaven, since it seems wonderful.

I don't remember when it happened, but Mamãe got a job. She got a job as a cleaning lady at a place that I think was a factory. It was a rectangular building, and in the middle was a little courtyard. I helped her clean the bathrooms. I thought I was super competent at scrubbing, mopping, and carrying buckets of water. I don't know if I was mostly in her way. I was five or six years old, and I would run around in the factory. She had told me that it was very important that I not bother other people or get in the way. If I did, she would lose the job, and we wouldn't have money for food. When I wasn't running around saying hello to everyone or helping my mother, I was in that little courtyard playing in the dirt.

One day, a man came up to me. He was white and older, and I recognized him. He was the man who had given her the job and who had said it was OK for her to bring me to work. I don't know if he owned the factory or if he was just the manager, but there he was, smiling at me. He greeted me nicely and asked me what I was up to. I pointed to the dirt in front of me and said I was playing. Then I quickly added that I would clean up after myself when I was done. He laughed a little and said I didn't need to worry. He started asking me more questions about how I was doing, how things were going for my mother, if I thought it was fun being here. It was a flood of questions that I answered politely. I was careful to answer that my mother and I were doing very well, that everyone was super nice, and that we were so happy and grateful to have a job. He asked me if I really understood how important it was for my mother that she had this job, how important it was for us.

I responded that I understood that and that we were grateful. The man kept talking, and I started to have this sneaking sense of discomfort. He said that my mother would be sad and angry if I did anything bad that led to her not being able to work there anymore. I felt embarrassed and wanted to ask him if I could go, but I didn't know if that would be impolite. Finally, the man asked me if I wanted a lollipop. I said yes.

My mother was on her knees, scrubbing the bathroom floor when I found her. She looked up at me smiling, but her smile quickly vanished.

"Christiana, what is it?" she asked.

"It's nothing, Mamãe. Do you want me to help you?" I asked.

She scrutinized me, giving me that look she usually gave me when she was trying to see through me.

I looked away. She came over to me and asked if someone had hurt me. I thought about what the man had said, how my mother and I needed this job and the money. It was my fault. But she didn't give up until I finally admitted I had tasted the man's "lollipop."

Mamãe's and my eyes met. She was giving me a strange look. She looked angry and sad, and I felt like I'd made a mistake. I started crying, and she hugged me and picked me up in her arms. That was something she didn't usually do anymore, because I'd gotten so big. I wasn't a baby anymore, as she often said.

Mamãe walked out of that bathroom, leaving the cleaning supplies there and—with me in her arms—she walked straight out of that factory, and we never went back. After she carried me for a while, we sat down, and then she asked me to tell her everything.

I apologized and said it was my fault and that I wouldn't do it again. I didn't actually know what it was that I'd done, but whatever it was, I wouldn't do it again. Mamãe explained to me that it wasn't my fault, that I hadn't done anything wrong. The man was the one who'd done something wrong, and we wouldn't be going back to that job. She told me that you had to be careful with men, that they were not as nice as women.

Life away from the protective shelter of our caves was like coming to a whole new world. The rules for survival were different out here. I realized very quickly that I had to adapt and learn the rules of life on the streets. One misstep could easily result in that being the last thing I ever did. When I remember what happened to me at that factory and what that man did to the child Christiana, I choose to remember the good in the situation. To be clear, there was nothing beautiful or good in what he did to me. We can easily ruin another person's life forever with our wicked and egotistical actions. But rather than the evil of the incident, I have chosen to carry with me what my mother did. What strength it must have taken for her to just pick me up and walk away from there, when we so desperately needed the money! She took the time to help me understand that what had happened wasn't my fault. It was bad, what had happened, but as I grew up, I took with me my mother's love instead of that man's ill will. I believe that has made all the difference. At the same time, I can't help but think of all the girls and women who have been and are being exploited and who don't have anyone to show them the way. Living with what happened hasn't been pain-free, but I have had love to counterbalance the evil. What happens if you only have the evil to bear?

Returning to Another World

2015

I'm sitting on a plane, somewhere between London and São Paulo. In less than ten hours, I will touch down in my home country for the first time in twenty-four years. In less than ten hours, my life will take a new turn. I suppose it already has. The turn happened three or four months ago when I decided to start digging into the past. I can't stop wondering when I began this journey. Maybe it was twenty-four years ago when I was adopted and ended up in the little village of Vindeln, in the middle of the forests of northern Sweden. I've always known that one day I would go back. A part of me thought it would happen sooner, that I wouldn't wait until I was thirty-two years old. At the same time, I know that I wasn't ready until now. A vaguely snarky voice in my head asks, "And are you ready now?"

I brush it aside. I look at the little yellow notebook in front of me, a present from Rivia who's sitting in the airplane seat next to me.

People often discuss going home again with me. Mostly out of curiosity. They're trying to understand how it feels to belong to two different cultures and wondering how it felt to make such a big change in my life, moving to a new country at the age of eight. Sometimes I feel like I hear something a little more loaded in the question. Am I not planning to leave Sweden and move back home? Sometimes I have the sense that the person is suggesting that it would be best if I did that. Thank goodness this doesn't happen very often. When I'm asked, "But haven't you ever thought about moving home to Brazil?" I don't know what to say. Not because I don't know if I want to, but rather because it's so odd. My home for the last twenty-four years has been northern Sweden. I mean, I'm Swedish. That's my home.

What would home be for me in Brazil? The cave? The favela? The streets? The orphanage? I'm quite certain that the folks at the orphanage no longer think I belong there. My home, right now anyway, is in Sweden. Who knows, maybe in ten years my home will be in the US or Australia or Norway. My home is where I'm happy, where I feel safe, where my friends and family are. My home is where I work and where I *feel* at home.

I have no idea if I'll feel at home when I step off this plane. But since I decided to return, memories have been coming back to me stronger and stronger. A kind of longing to see the caves again has even taken root. Maybe what feels the most like home to me in Brazil are the little caves in the wilderness outside Diamantina that my mother and I lived in. I don't really know what to do with all these thoughts, questions, and memories swirling in my head.

I turn off my overhead light and close my eyes.

Some Scars Never Leave the Body

São Paulo, Brazil, 1989

We were standing in an open-air market. We were going to buy food. There were big, red tomatoes, and my mouth was watering. I reached out my hand to take one, but the vendor slapped my hand away. Mamãe found some other tomatoes in a box on the ground and picked up the worst-looking one. They were moldy and soft in places. I asked my mother why she was taking the bad tomatoes. She smiled a little sadly and said, "Christiana, look at this tomato. One side is bad, but what do you think happens if we cut away the bad parts?"

Mamãe always did that. When she wanted to teach me something, she had me answer questions. I looked at the tomato and said, "If we cut off the bad parts, the goodish ones are left."

She smiled and continued. "It's the same with people. Don't forget it! Why don't these tomatoes deserve to be eaten? Why are they so much worse than the others? Don't you think they'd be just as good in a stew as the pretty ones? If all tomatoes are just going to be eaten up, do you think it makes any difference what they look like beforehand? They'll all be cooked one way or another."

I still wanted to get the nice-looking tomatoes.

She smiled again and said, "You deserve the best, my dear, but today we have to settle for the less pretty ones."

While she bought the ugly tomatoes, I tried to understand why all the tomatoes needed to end up in the stew. The pretty tomatoes would surely be bought by rich, white people whereas Mamãe and I, who didn't have enough money, would have to settle for the bad ones. It was always like that. White people had money, and they could always afford to buy what they wanted. I tried to understand why life was like that. Did God want it to be like that? It didn't feel fair. I mean, God was supposed to be good. But how could God be good if we always got the bad tomatoes?

Suddenly, I heard my mother and another woman yelling at each other. Mamãe was angry, and so was the other woman. I didn't understand what the fuss was about, but I got scared. I'd hardly ever seen my mother truly angry, but now she was. I heard her yelling to me, "Christiana, take Patrique!" and suddenly she let go of my brother. Out of sheer reflex, I reached out my arms and managed to catch him just before he hit the asphalt. Mamãe and the white lady were fighting, and I didn't understand why. I wanted to yell at them to stop, but I couldn't get any words to come out. Two policemen ran up and separated them. The white woman explained something to the policemen, and Mamãe looked terribly angry. The policeman let go of the other woman, and Mamãe said something that I understood was somewhat insulting. One of the policemen slapped her face.

I got so mad that I forgot I was holding my little brother in my arms. I ran forward and kicked the policeman on the shin and hit him as hard as I could in the stomach with my right fist. The second policeman grabbed me, and I almost dropped Patrique. The policeman held on to me tightly while the other one, the one I'd kicked, came over and looked at me with hatred in his eyes. It really scared me, but I tried not to show it. He raised his machine gun and hit me right on the jaw with it. I heard the crack in my mouth and my panic-stricken mother screaming my name. I tasted blood in my mouth, and as I collapsed, I thought, *Don't drop Patrique . . .*

That wasn't the first time I'd been roughed up by the police, and it wouldn't be the last. Even today, I have trouble with my jaw. Some scars never leave the body.

That incident at the marketplace ended behind bars on a concrete floor.

It was nighttime, and I was cold. Mamãe held me. I apologized to her for hitting the policeman. I felt like it was my fault that we were sitting where we were. She said it wasn't my fault, that this was just how the world and life worked. I asked her if this was how God wanted the world to work, for us to be beaten and hurt and unhappy. My mother never answered that question, but she made me promise that if she wasn't there, if I was alone, that I would always run and hide when I saw the police. We sat in silence for a bit. I had a bad feeling in the pit of my stomach.

"Mamãe, you'll never leave me, right?"

She eyed me sadly, put her hand on my chest, and said, "I will never leave you. I will always be here with you, in your heart. I'm a part of you. I'm inside you, and if you ever feel sad or lost, I'll be there with you. Don't forget it."

I woke up to the sound of a policeman chatting with my mother. I heard him say something to her along the lines of "Either you or your daughter, you decide."

She didn't answer him, just gently repositioned the upper half of my body, which had been resting on her lap, onto the concrete floor and asked me to hold Patrique. "I'll be back soon," she said. I asked her where she was going, but she shushed me and said I shouldn't worry. "Haven't I always come back to you?" she asked, and smiled. Her smile seemed forced. I know she could see how worried I was. I looked from her to the police officer and back to her. I heard how he impatiently asked her to go with him. She stood up, and before she turned around, I saw her eyes change. She looked strong.

I knew what was going to happen. Although I didn't understand everything, I understood that the policeman was going to hurt her. What had he said? "Either you or your daughter . . ." It was my fault we were sitting in here, and it was my fault she was forced to go off with the policeman. *Please, please, God. Let me be big and strong when I grow up! Let me be big and strong so I can stop bad men, like policemen, from hurting the people I love.* Patrique started crying. I rocked him back and forth. I wanted to quiet him so Mamãe wouldn't need to worry. I wanted to show her that I could take care of him when she wasn't around. I wondered if Patrique understood what was going on. I wondered if he could somehow sense that I was upset and that they were going to hurt Mamãe, and I thought, *I love you, little brother, and no one is going to hurt you! I promise.*

I don't know how long I waited for my mother to come back. Patrique fell asleep, and I sat on that cold concrete floor, my back against the wall. I remember one of my butt cheeks and my leg had fallen asleep, but I was afraid to move. I didn't want to wake up my little brother, so I sat there and tried not to think about what was happening behind that closed door. After what felt like forever, that same policeman came back in with Mamãe. Looking very satisfied, he glanced at me and smiled a creepy smile that made me feel little, scared, and disgusted inside.

When I asked Mamãe what had happened, she said they had just asked her a few questions about what had really happened at the market, that it was nothing I needed to worry about, and that everything would look better in the morning. That was the first time I felt like my mother really lied to me. I didn't want to do anything that would upset her more or make her worry, so I lay down on the floor with Patrique's head on my arm and brought him to my chest so I could keep him warm. Although I lay close to Mamãe, I turned my back to her and curled up in a fetal position. I wanted her to feel my love, but somehow I understood that she needed some space and a little time to recover. I pretended to be asleep. I lay awake almost the entire night. I could hear her breathing, and I knew she was crying.

The tears of the powerless are not tears of frustration. They're not tears that gush or tears that burn. The tears of the powerless are silent and resigned. When you know that no one cares, the tears are all you have. You need them to be able to go on, to be able to feel hope, because they relieve the pressure. I know that these tears can make all the difference in the world to a six-year-old who needs her mother's love. My mother cried these tears many times. Even if it was awful, I now understand, as a grown-up, that it's good if you can cry. Even though there aren't any tears in the world, visible or invisible, that can make what is wrong right, especially for the powerless.

I lay awake for a long time and prayed to God to make my mother happy and to let us out of the police station. In my powerlessness, that was the only thing I could do. I prayed to God that I could think of a way to scrounge a little money the next day, to buy Mamãe something nice. Maybe that could make her forget this awful night, forget the powerlessness and how it had yet again shown the strength it possessed and the marks it left behind. Patrique woke up a few times during the night, and some of those times my mother carefully took him from my arms and nursed him. Then she gave him back to me.

I understood that she needed more time. I took Patrique and remained lying with my back to my mother so she could have a little peace. I looked at my little brother. He was so cute, but he smelled like a mix of baby, pee, and poop. My eyes wandered over to Mamãe. I didn't want to bother her. She understood what I wanted, though, because she gave me a piece of cloth without any words being spoken. I took the cloth, turned around, and continued to keep my back to her. Patrique was good. He didn't cry or scream. I undid the towel he was wrapped in. He didn't have any clothes, just a cloth diaper. I unclipped the safety pin holding his cloth diaper closed, opened the diaper, and tried to wipe away as much of the poop as possible with the dry bits of his old diaper. I set him on the new piece of cloth. When I had that on him, I wrapped him back up in the towel. I laid his body against mine and watched as he fell asleep. He was the most beautiful baby I'd ever seen, and he was mine and Mamãe's. When he cried, I would sometimes laugh at him since he looked like a wrinkly old man, a very cute, angry, wrinkly old man. I kissed him on the cheek and then tried to sleep.

Thoughts Aswirl

2015

The sound of the pilot's voice in my headphones wakes me up, and immediately my brain gets to work.

I know that a part of me is on my way home. Christiana is on her way home. But Christina is leaving home. I suppose that's how I felt all those years in Sweden: part of me wanted to go home, and part of me *was* home. I can't say for sure how I'll feel after this emotionally charged trip, but I have a hard time believing I won't feel like I'm coming home when I land in Sweden again. And how will I feel when I land in Brazil? Like I've come home? I understand that the country has changed since my time there—I hope for the better. I understand that over time, all places, people, and cultures change, but most of all, we change. I'm not the same person I was then. Just knowing that I'm sitting on this plane, somewhere over the Atlantic, and will land in less than ten hours makes me slightly hysterical.

Before I left Sweden, I went into overdrive with all the preparations, and I haven't really allowed myself to let out my thoughts and feelings. I've always been a bit of a control freak, and I try to bring some order to my thoughts, try to be aware of what my expectations are, and prepare myself for what I may encounter. I don't believe that this is about coming home again, but I hope that maybe I'll be able to build another home. I hope that I'll feel at home in Brazil. I hope that I'll get to meet my biological mother, and I hope that in the future I'll be able to have two homes. I've always loved Brazil, even from afar and despite all the bad things that happened to me there. Maybe I'm more worried that I won't feel at home at all, that I won't fit in or will stop feeling the positive feelings for the country and the people that I've carried inside me for so many years. What happens to all my memories and feelings if my experiences from this trip are exclusively negative? Will the love and joy that I feel disappear if, as an adult, I don't feel any affinity with the land of my birth? I tell myself to stop thinking about it since I can't change whatever will be. After all, I decided to put myself through this. But that doesn't mean I'm in control of the situation. I sigh. *OK, Christina, when you get like this, it's because you're afraid. So, what are you actually most afraid of?* I take a piece of paper and a pen and write down two questions for myself, as I've learned to do when everything feels out of control:

What is the goal of my trip?

What am I hoping for?

I start with the first question. The goal is to travel back into my past, to the joy and the sorrow, and confront it. The goal is to visit the orphanage and the slums and the streets where I lived. To find the caves where I spent my first years, and to find my family, especially my mother.

What am I hoping for? I draw a complete blank—I can't answer this question at all. But that can't be right. Obviously, I know what I'm hoping for! Fear of what I will find makes it almost impossible for me to express my hope in words.

I hope to see my mother . . . As I write this, I feel something catch. *I hope I'll see my mother.* Something doesn't feel entirely genuine in what I've written. It feels like I wrote what should be obvious, but the obvious may not be what I really feel. I sense my stress level rise; my body starts to feel hot. Am I a bad person? Of course, I want to find my mother—why wouldn't I want to? I mean, I've been without her, missed her, for twenty-four years. She took care of me, did her best, gave me love, sacrificed herself for me. Is this how I show my gratitude, my love? I turn the question over in my mind. *Do you want your mother to be dead?* The answer is an immediate no. No, I don't want my mother to be dead. When I think about it, I am 100 percent certain that that is not what I want. To the contrary, I've been afraid for a long time that I would return to Brazil and find out that if I'd only come back a few years earlier, I would have seen her again.

I mull things over for a while and finally realize that I'm afraid of what will happen if I find her. I already know what happens if I don't. My life will continue as it has so far. I've lived without her for all these years. I've lived without my adoptive mother for sixteen years, missing her. If I find out my biological mother has passed away, I already know what the rest of my life will consist of. It will be more years of missing her. But that won't change very much. It will be almost the way it is now. I can handle my life the way it is now. On the other hand, what scares me about the possibility of finding out she's alive and being able to see her again after twenty-four years is suddenly having a mother after sixteen years without one. I exhale.

Somewhere in all these thoughts and feelings, I sense that I've found the root of my fear. If Mamãe is alive and we find her, I might have to accept that she might not want anything to do with me. Instinctively, however, I realize that deep down, I don't believe that. I think of all the times she hugged me, said I was special, that she loves me, and all the laughter and tears we've shared. If Mamãe is alive, I don't need to worry about her not wanting to see me. So, what am I afraid of? What if she's disappointed in me? But I don't believe that's the problem, either. I suddenly realize the problem is me! I'm afraid of the consequences. It's hard to admit this, because it's a selfish thought. How will it affect my life if she's alive? How is she doing? Where does she live? What condition is she in? Does she need looking after, and if she does, can I afford it?

How can we make a life work when she lives in Brazil and I have my life in Sweden? How will we communicate when I don't speak Portuguese anymore and she doesn't speak a word of Swedish? What happens when Rivia isn't there to interpret? What if seeing each other doesn't result in any positive feelings, only negative ones? I have no idea what problems could arise or how I would handle them. It feels like it's my turn to handle the problems, my turn to take care of her.

I have no idea what the future will bring if I find my mother, and that's frightening. I realize that none of what I've written matters. All that matters is knowing why I'm scared. And that I'm suppressing a homesickness that a part of me has felt for so many years. I can make do with that. I'll leave the rest to the future, because whatever will be, will be. I put away my pen and turn off my overhead light. I put my headphones on and decide to watch a feel-good movie. There are eight hours left until we land and my brain is tired, but I'm far too exhilarated to sleep.

Camile, My Very First Friend
São Paulo, 1989–1991

I can't tell you for sure how I met the girl who became my very first friend. I wish I could tell you a lovely, funny story about the first time we met. About how fate brought us together, how the adventure began, and how we forged a strong bond of friendship. But I really can't remember how she came into my life. It fascinates me that I can't remember how I met the person who would go on to be so important to me, who would change my life forever. Maybe it isn't so odd that I can't remember. After all, it's impossible to know that the person you're meeting for the first time is someone you will end up loving.

Camile is the name of the girl I came to love as a sister. I'm positive that we met in the favela, and I know that through her, I met other kids and found a sense of belonging to a group of friends. I can't say exactly how long I got to have her in my life, whether our friendship lasted for two months or a year. I didn't know what time was, just that after every night came a new day. I knew the days had names and the order they came in, but I didn't know that a month was four weeks long or that there were fifty-two weeks in a year. What I have left of my time with Camile is the memory of various events and things we did together. I have no idea how long we did them or when.

Camile was a very special girl. She was what I would now call an old soul. Talking to her was sometimes like talking to a grown-up. She could be scary-smart, and she knew things that the rest of us didn't know. She was a bit older than I was and very pretty. She was unbelievably nice and had the ability to captivate adults and children when she told her stories. Oh, how Camile loved to tell stories. Her eyes would twinkle, and her body language would change. She had theories about all sorts of things. She usually saw things from a new and different perspective. That was what I loved most about Camile. We complemented each other: I was curious and mischievous, and she was wise and stable. I dragged her along on adventures, and she stopped them from ending in disaster. When I think of Camile, it's with warmth and love, laughter and tears.

As an adult, I've come to understand that the relationships I've sought out and built in Sweden have their foundations in what Camile gave me: a friendship based on trust, security, warmth, and respect.

Camile didn't usually talk about her parents. It was obvious that she didn't want to talk about them. Whenever we ran into someone who asked her about her parents, she usually just said she didn't have any. She never looked sad or made a big deal about it. She simply kept talking as if she'd just answered any old question. But I could tell from her voice that it was a tough subject for her. One evening, we were sitting under the little staircase where we sometimes slept. I asked her about her mother and father. She pulled up her T-shirt and showed me a huge scar that ran from her back to her stomach. Then she said that she didn't have any parents. I remember that I felt for her. At least I had a mother who loved me and tried to take care of me. So, I gave her my banana. She looked a little sad when she accepted the banana and said that if all she had to do to get food was show people her scar, then she'd walk around without a shirt every day. We laughed, and she broke the banana in two and gave me half.

During our time together, we made several pacts. We decided to always share the food we found, begged for, or stole. Camile explained to me that this doubled our chances of having food on any given day. We also promised to always help each other if one of us ever wound up in trouble. That's how Camile was. She taught me what friendship is.

With the Trash

The interesting thing about memory is that you don't always remember how you got to a point or what happened after it. You just know you were there. I know that on this one day this one time, Camile and I were going through the trash at a garbage dump. We were looking for toys, clothes, and anything at all that seemed like something we could use ourselves or could barter with someone else. Camile found a soccer ball that looked very worn, and I found a big, thin metal wheel that was maybe a bicycle wheel. I dug for a while longer and finally found what I was looking for: a long stick.

I showed Camile my find. She was clutching her soccer ball while I stood up my wheel, holding it upright with the stick. I looked at Camile. She smiled, and I started running, rolling the wheel along in front of me. It was tricky to keep the wheel balanced using the stick, and you couldn't make any sharp turns because the wheel would fall. After I played with the wheel for a while, Camile wanted to try, too. I took her soccer ball, and she started running. I ran next to her. After a while, she set aside the wheel and started playing with the soccer ball. Barefoot, we kicked the ball back and forth between us. Neither of us had any control over how we kicked it, but we were having so much fun. We pretended that we were on the national team, that we were famous and that everyone wanted to be like us. We were trying to learn to get the ball airborne when we kicked it. In one of my first attempts to get the ball off the ground, I managed to kick it so hard that it rolled away, toward some boys who were at the garbage dump. One of them took the ball and called to two of his buddies that he'd found something. Camile and I ran over to the boys and said it was our ball. The boy holding the ball said that he'd found it, so the ball was his. I walked over and tried to take it, but he pushed me away. I yelled at him that it was our ball.

Camile didn't get into fights very often. She would turn a blind eye to things that I found unfair, something I had a hard time doing. On those occasions when Camile did end up in a fight, it was usually because she had to, to help me. Afterward, I would often discover that she was mad at me, especially the times she ended up with bruises all over her body.

This day was one of those times. I got so mad. That boy was standing there with our ball under his arm. I walked over to him and punched him as hard as I could in the stomach. I managed to get another hit in before the other boys flew at me. Camile started fighting, too, and all of us were rolling around, trying to get in as many punches as we could. When we were finished, or rather when Camile and I had lost the fight, the boys stood up and we sat down on the ground. One of them turned around to see where the ball was. Two new guys were holding the ball. They looked like they were probably about fourteen or fifteen. The ball thief yelled at one of the guys that the ball was his. The guys laughed and said, "Come and take it, then!"

The boy realized there wasn't a chance in the world that he would be able to get it back. One of the older boys yelled at the younger ones to get lost. They left, and then Camile and I stood up. The two older guys came toward us. The guy holding the ball held it out to me, winked, and smiled.

"Here's your ball, cutie," he said, and then laughed until he and his buddy walked away.

I blushed, and a wave of warmth spread through me. It was like sugar around my heart.

"Camile, he said I was cute."

"He must be blind," she said, looking at me disapprovingly. "How can you be cute when you're covered in bruises all the time and have a split lip?" She turned away in a huff and trudged off.

I followed her, smiling. After a bit, I ran and caught up to her. I knew she was mad at me, but I stuck my tongue out and threw the ball to her. She caught it. I grabbed the metal wheel and the stick, and we walked back to the garbage dump. I never said this out loud to Camile, but I remember I felt really foolish for having started that fight, especially since it had been so obvious who was going to come out on top. Without a doubt, I was the more childish of the two of us.

Certain moments among my memories fill me with joy. That snapshot image, when we were playing and a boy told me I was cute, is one of those moments. Many others I'd rather not remember.

Why Do You Hurt Us Like This, God?

There were times when I woke up feeling like it would be a good day. Other mornings, I knew right away that something was off, and thoughts about what kind of misery was going to unfold would hound me the whole day. This was one of those mornings, and Camile was irritated with me for being so negative. I was complaining about everything, from why we lived in this filthy part of the city to why God hated us. I wondered why we girls always had to suffer most and why I constantly had to go hungry. My complaining continued for a good long while.

Santos, who was hanging out with us on this morning, quickly got fed up with my complaining and told Camile that we should come find him when I was in a better mood. Santos was the first boy I really liked. He was a few years older and was always extra nice to me. He dreamed of becoming an airplane mechanic or a pilot. Of course, like so many other street children, he also dreamed of becoming one of the world's best soccer players. Santos lived in the favela with his mother and stepfather in a little shanty. I met him through Camile, and sometimes we all hung out together and got into mischief. After Santos ran off, I kept droning on to Camile, feeling sorry for myself and complaining about how unfair life was. Suddenly, she crossed her arms and scowled at me.

"You're such a ray of sunshine today, my little *libélula,* my little firefly! If we're lucky, you'll scare away half the slum, and we'll get to keep everything for ourselves." The sarcasm in her voice was obvious, which annoyed me even more.

We were walking in silence down the narrow walkways between the shanty houses when suddenly a man came toward us. As we went to pass him, he stood right in front of us and leered one of those gross grins you only see from drunk, horny men. We tried to go around him on the side, but he blocked our way again. In her very firm voice, which always made her sound older than she was, Camile told the man to move out of the way so we could pass. He eyed her with a scornful, haughty look and said, "You're not going anywhere today, my beautiful girls. You're coming with me!" As he said it, he took a firm hold of Camile's arm.

She tried to get free. I kicked him in the shin as hard as I could while Camile bit his hand. He let go of Camile, but then grabbed me by the hair instead. I screamed. It felt like he was ripping my head in two. I saw Camile pick up a wooden board that was leaning against one of the shanties. She ran at the man and hit him hard on the head, and I felt him release his hold on my hair. Neither Camile nor I waited around to see if he was hurt. We did what we'd done so many times before. We ran as fast as we could. Camile ran in front of me, leading the way. I looked back and saw that the man was following us. I screamed to Camile that he was coming. Camile turned right, then right again, then left. She kept going straight ahead. I was glad she was leading the way, because I had absolutely no sense of direction. Suddenly, she stopped and started pounding on a door.

"Marina, open up. Please, open the door!" She kept pounding.

"Camile, he's coming!" I screamed at her.

"Marina, *open up!*"

I had no idea who Marina was, but if Camile trusted her, that was good enough for me. The door opened, and Camile and I ran inside and slammed it shut.

"What happened? Camile, what happened?" the woman in the room asked, looking very concerned.

"A man . . . he's . . . after . . . us . . . ," Camile responded in between gasps for breath.

There was a pounding on the door. "Let me in! I know you're in there, you little whores!"

"Quick, hide!" the woman whispered.

Marina's little shack, like most of the places in the slums, had only one room. We hid behind some kind of counter, and Marina opened the door. She didn't even have a chance to say anything before the man pushed his way into the room past her.

"Where are those little devils?" he hollered drunkenly.

"Which ones? If you mean those girls, they're gone now."

"The hell they are! You're hiding them. Look what they did to me!"

Camile and I looked at each other. When a man was this angry, it never ended well. We exchanged frightened looks. It was only a matter of time until he found us.

"You're not interested in a couple of little girls when there's a full-grown woman in front of you, are you?" Marina's voice had changed and suddenly sounded much gentler, more appealing. Camile and I looked at each other, knowing that it was our fault that this was happening and that Marina would suffer for it.

"Take off your clothes!" the man ordered.

Both Camile and I put our hands over our ears, but the disgusting moans from the man and the degrading words he said to Marina forced their way through our hands. No matter how hard I tried to close my eyes and imagine something else, I heard him. When he was done, Camile and I thought we'd finally be able to leave our hiding spot, but he didn't leave. After a few hours, we heard Marina scream and then the man's voice.

"You women are nothing but whores!"

We sat there, pressing our hands over our ears and squeezing our eyes shut. He finally left. Camile and I sat quietly. We looked at each other, wondering what we should do. After a while, Marina said we could come out. She'd put on her clothes, made the bed, and was acting like nothing had happened, but we could see that she was sad. Her cheek was swollen, and we saw how her hands trembled as she tried to put all the things back where they'd been.

"I'm going to make some coffee. Would you girls like some?"

"Yes, please," Camile replied quietly, timidly.

While Marina made the coffee, I looked around the room. On a little table in one corner stood a statue of the Virgin Mary. Her head was bowed, and her arms were outstretched in a welcoming embrace. Her heart was visible: it was red, and a ring of thorny branches formed a circle around it. There were several candles in front of the statue, and Marina had hung a rosary around it.

I didn't know anyone in the slums who wasn't a believer. At least they all claimed they were. I assume you've got to believe in something when no one believes in themselves. Maybe people just need to find a way to get through the day. I didn't think before I spoke and just blurted out, "Why do you hurt us like this, God?" Camile gave me a stern look. *Shut up.* I turned around, and Marina was looking at me.

"God doesn't want us to be happy. He wants us to survive. One day, you'll understand!" When my eyes met Marina's, I saw something there, or rather, I saw something that wasn't there. She was one step closer to becoming a ghost, like my mother had told me. And what had happened today was Camile's and my fault.

Marina turned away and got out three cups. We all sat in silence and drank coffee, as if nothing had happened, as if this were just part of everyday life.

The Boy Santos

The slum is like an independent state within the state, kind of like the Vatican but with God missing. It's downright ironic, I sometimes think, because the slums are where people's faith in God is the greatest.

There aren't very many people inside the slum who care what happens outside the slum, just like how most people who live outside the slum don't care that the slum exists. It's hard for some people who were born in the slum to advance and get anywhere in life. "Advancement" in the slum is becoming a gang leader, which often results in a short life.

I remember getting chills every time I came up against gang members or their leaders. It was pretty much only guys who joined the gangs. Sometimes you saw a girl who was in one, and everyone knew why she was there. Girl gang members shared more or less the same background: no parents, no family, no money, and nowhere to live. It was incredibly hard to protect yourself against boys and men if you didn't have an adult or a gang looking out for you. Being raped, over and over, by men who didn't care what kind of violence they used was significantly more dangerous than letting some of the guys in the gang have sex with you. Or being one of their girlfriends. This way, the girls were mostly "protected" from the rest of the street.

Life could be terrible even for those who did have a grown-up around. A grown-up wasn't at all a guarantee of protection. I remember one little girl who was somewhere between seven and nine. She was wearing a dirty dark-red dress that was too big for her. She was sitting on a chair outside a shack in the slum. Her hair, cut short, about to her ears, was sticking out in every direction. She was barefoot and had dark eyes. I don't know why she's stuck in my memory. Maybe it was the contrast between her small body and that big, dirty red dress, or between her vacant stare and her cute face. There was something special about her, because I can still picture her. I never talked to her, and our eyes only met one time. On a table in front of her was a white pack of cigarettes, and between her fingers she was holding a lit one. She sat with one leg on the chair, and the dress revealed the breasts she didn't have. It wasn't that unusual for us kids to run around without clothes on. But on her, it seemed so wrong to see her naked torso.

Seated cross-legged, I was leaning against the shack across from her, waiting for Camile, when a man opened the door behind the girl. He came out in just underpants and seemed drunk. He looked at the girl, grabbed her by the hair, pulled her up off the chair, and yanked her into the shack. She didn't scream or cry. You could tell she was used to being treated that way. It was always awful to see someone in the slums who'd become a ghost, who was no longer responsive, who didn't feel anything, who merely existed but didn't really live.

I know that I sat there thinking about whether what I'd just seen was what I could expect out of life. I must have looked sad, because when Camile came back, she asked how I was doing. I just stood up and said I'd seen a ghost. She nodded in understanding, and we wandered off. Camile understood right away what I'd seen.

One night, I was sitting with Camile, Santos, Angelo, and Javier around a fire pit. We were sharing a barbecued chicken. Angelo and Javier were brothers, about seven and five years old, and they lived near Santos. What I remember about these two boys is that they wanted to be cool. They were very funny and imaginative. They asked Camile to tell them a story. Every time we met up with them, as soon as they were around her, they wanted to hear a story.

It had been a good day that had ended with Santos's mother making us dinner. Javier and Angelo started nagging Camile, who just smiled. It didn't take long before Santos and I also chimed in, asking Camile to tell us a story.

"OK! What kind of story do you want?" Camile said, pretending to feel put-upon.

"A scary story!" Javier exclaimed.

"Then you'll just get scared and have nightmares," Angelo teased his little brother.

"I will not!"

"You will, too!"

"OK, I'll tell you a story that's also a riddle, but only if you two promise to be quiet the whole time," Camile said, giving the brothers a stern but amused look.

Santos's and my eyes met, and we smiled. It was hard not to laugh whenever the brothers, Javier and Angelo, started arguing.

"Are you ready?" Camile asked. "It's pretty tricky."

"Yes!" we all responded in unison.

"Once upon a time, there were two brothers, Paulo and Pedro. Paulo always did the right thing. He was nice and helpful, but he always had an ulterior motive for what he did. Pedro, on the other hand, was naughty. He never helped anyone, he grabbed stuff for himself, and he hit people. But he was always sorry afterward. Now, my question to you is, Which was the bad one, Paulo or Pedro?"

"Pedro," Javier and Angelo agreed.

Camile looked at Santos and me. "And what do you guys think?"

"It's obvious. It's not hard at all," Santos replied. "Paulo must be the bad one!"

"What do you say?" Camile asked me.

"Hmm . . . ," I said, eyeing Camile. I knew it wasn't as easy as it sounded. It never was with Camile's riddles. "I think both the brothers are equally bad and equally good. Paulo behaves well, but in his heart, he's bad. Pedro hurts people, but he doesn't actually want to hurt them."

When I was done, it was quiet for a moment. Everyone was looking at me, and I got the sense that I'd solved the riddle. That sense didn't last long, though, because Santos started laughing, and then Javier and

Angelo joined in. We were sitting in front of the fire pit in the night-time darkness. Santos threw a chicken bone at me, and we all started laughing. Santos said something about how I was always being different and that I was wrong.

I looked at Camile, who blew me a kiss and smiled. Then I knew I had solved the riddle.

If the others hadn't also been able to see Camile, I'd have thought she was an angel come down from heaven to be my friend.

That night we slept content, all together, our bellies full.

In the morning, a noise from the shack where Santos lived woke us up. We could hear things breaking and a scream from inside. Camile had slept in the hammock with the brothers, and Santos and I slept along the outside wall with some blankets over us.

I sat up and pulled my legs in against my body. I looked at Santos and saw him press his head against the wall and close his eyes. Each time something broke or when we heard his mother get hit, his body jerked.

I looked at Camile. She had gotten up and had her arms around Angelo and Javier. Camile looked at me, and none of us knew what to do.

"Santos, I'm sorry . . . ," I began.

"Leave it!" His voice sounded hard.

Camile sat down next to him and put her arm around him.

Santos shook her off and stood up. "He's a fucking idiot! He can't do anything right. All he does is hit her. I hate him!"

"Santos, should we go somewhere else?" I asked a little hesitantly. The argument was heating up, and I found it tough to listen to. How hard must it have been for Santos?

"I'm not going anywhere except in there!" He started walking toward the door, but Camile stopped him.

"You can't go in there. He'll kill you! He's drunk. I'm sure he'll fall asleep soon."

Santos shoved Camile aside. "If he kills me, then he's doing me a favor!" Santos opened the door to the shack, walked in, and slammed it hard behind himself.

Camile, Angelo, Javier, and I remained outside, and we realized that no good could come of this. Santos would probably be beaten so badly that he wouldn't be able to move for a good long while. His mother would definitely be punished for having given birth to a son like him and maybe be forced to kick him out. Camile looked at me. We were all feeling helpless.

What had presumably driven Santos into the shack was that his mother was getting hit over and over. It became too much for him. This had been going on for a long time. His stepfather hit his mother, and Santos himself was always covered in bruises. He used to say that the only reason he stuck around home was that he didn't want to leave his mother alone with that idiot. Maybe he felt guilty about not having done anything about it; he definitely felt powerless. Anyhow, I know that's how we all felt as we stood there hearing it all. We wanted to help him, but we didn't know how. After all, we were just kids. We could have all run in there together and attacked the man, but then what? How would that improve anything for Santos and his mother? So we did the only thing we could—we just stood there and listened. We stuck around in case Santos needed us. We didn't want to abandon him; he was one of us, a part of the family. Suddenly, we heard a man's voice.

"And just what do you think you're going to do with that, you son of bitch? You're not man enough to even hold something like that, and you're definitely not man enough to use it."

Silence followed, and then there was a sound, a sound we all knew well. It made us all jump, and our hearts beat faster. There was no doubt about it: it was a gunshot. I looked at Camile in horror, and the look on her face must have mirrored mine. The silence was broken by a woman's scream. Camile, the brothers, and I instinctively backed away from the shack.

"Santos," I whispered to Camile, and she just stared at me. She didn't know whether he was alive, either. Neither of us dared say any more.

The door opened, and out came Santos. He looked at us in fear, determination in his eyes, and then he turned around and ran.

"What have you done? What have you done, Santos?" his mother screamed. She was sobbing hysterically, and it was scary to hear and see an adult act in such a weird and crazy way. People had started flocking toward the shack, and we kids realized it was time for us to get out of there. We knew what had happened.

What had started as a magical night ended in a new day that reminded us of our reality.

Santos was ten years old when he killed a man. I remember wondering whether Camile and I would ever do anything so horrible. I was about seven when that happened.

We tried to find Santos. We searched for several days, but no one seemed to know where he'd gone. He had just disappeared. I've always wondered how he's living his life today, *if* he's living at all. I wish he'd let us be there for him, but he chose to disappear and there was nothing we could do. I liked Santos, and I used to tell him we should get married when we grew up. He would hug me and say, "Sure, whatever you want!" and then he usually gave me a big smile.

I've always wondered what would be written on Santos's tombstone: *Santos, ten-year-old boy, killed the man who beat him and his mother, fled, disappeared. Murderer.*

Or: *Santos, ten-year-old boy, loved airplanes, wanted to be the best soccer player in the world. Missed. Hero.*

The Plane Touches Down Gently

São Paulo, 2015

Finally, we've landed at Guarulhos International Airport in São Paulo. Rivia and I are standing by the baggage claim carousel, waiting for our bags. The trip went well, and the plane touched down gently. My fear of flying peaks at landing, so I sent a grateful thought to the pilots. Rivia, who has a Brazilian passport, took the short line into the country while I waited in the incredibly long line that didn't seem to move forward at all. Standing in line is not my thing. And this particular line twisted and turned like the Great Wall of China through what felt like the whole airport. Wide and thick and impenetrable. Apparently, Swedes have a very advanced line-waiting culture. Swedish people are some of the best in the world at waiting in line, and over the years, I have learned to wait in lines. But it's hard for me. My early years in Brazil left their mark on me, and mostly I want to do this *jeitinho brasileiro*—the Brazilian way—which would probably look something like this: I would go up to whoever's at the front of the line and tell them a white lie about how I'm late for an appointment and ask if they might let me go ahead of them. I'm not proud to admit this, but as a kid I sometimes did that to avoid having to wait in line. As an adult, I clench my teeth and wait, realizing that everyone waiting in this line wishes they, too, were doing something else.

I'm tired. Outside the airport, the sun is just rising over São Paulo. I look around. I watch the people standing in the line and hear various languages. I get out my Swedish passport and look at my picture. After what feels like an eternity, it's my turn to step forward to one of the glass booths and show my passport to a dumpy woman who seems extremely bored. I smile and say hi in Portuguese, *"Oi,"* as I hand her my passport. She looks at the passport and then looks at me, at the passport again and back at me. She seems a little surprised and asks me something in Portuguese that I don't understand. I respond, *"Eu não falo português, fala inglês?"* She shakes her head, no, she doesn't speak English, and stamps my passport. Finally, I'm let into the country.

I see Rivia standing on the far side of the baggage carousel, and I start walking toward her. I bump into an elderly woman and want to apologize, but I don't know how to say that in Portuguese, so I say it in English. Already, I'm frustrated that I can't speak the language and embarrassed that I haven't taken the time to learn it. When I reach Rivia, I ask her how to say *excuse me* in Portuguese. *"Desculpe,"* she replies. Our bags come rolling out onto the carousel. Rivia picks up her light-green bag, while I awkwardly heave mine out backward, half stumbling. Rivia smiles. We wander out of the airport toward the taxis. Rivia arranges a car. We climb into the backseat and give the driver the address of the hotel where we're staying. It's in the Jardins neighborhood. As we get out onto the road, I start to recognize the vegetation, the bushes and trees, and even the smells and the traffic itself. Immediately I feel split in half. After twenty-four years, suddenly I'm back, as if no time has passed. And yet, so many years have gone by. An odd sensation slips over me, and I try to figure out what I'm really feeling.

I smile and point to things I recognize and things that, though they have been hidden away and forgotten, are now suddenly there in my head. We pass a police car, and I react immediately. I tell Rivia I don't like it. Some scars run way too deep.

We drive into the concrete city, and I see so many buildings with graffiti tags—none in color, just black spray-painted tags everywhere. It's unbelievably ugly, and I feel a disappointment that I try to hide. The city feels ugly and grimy and harsh. I don't want to see this. What if I've gotten so used to Swedish life that I can no longer face this? But the farther into the city the taxi brings us, the better it feels. The gloomy suburbs are replaced by a more charming downtown. After almost an hour's drive, we reach the hotel. We climb out of the taxi. Though it's sunny, the day is not as hot as I expected.

We leave our luggage with the front desk and go to breakfast. We each take a plate and start helping ourselves to bread, fruit, and pastries. Rivia points to some small, round rolls and tells me I have to taste them. I look at the balls and feel like I recognize them. Rivia says they're *pão de queijo*, cheese puffs. I take three of them and some mango and papaya. We sit down. The cheese puffs are amazing! I know that I ate them when I was little; I don't know when exactly, but I remember the taste. My mouth recognizes the taste. I go get more cheese puffs. It feels like I'm trying to eat Brazil.

An hour later, Rivia and I step out of the elevator and into the hotel lobby. After a long shower, I feel like a new person, and we decide to go see a little of São Paulo. We go to a famous park called Ibirapuera. We wander around and buy coconut water, and I feel a bit tipsy. I recognize the plants, palms, smells, and the language. The sun is warm in a familiar way, and even though I don't understand what the people around me are saying, the language is familiar.

It doesn't take more than fifteen minutes for me to find a tree and start climbing. I discover quickly that my jeans are way too tight for tree climbing, so I just sit in the tree for a while, until we see some guards heading toward us. I climb down, and we keep wandering.

We find two big walls of graffiti art that vastly surpass most of what we saw earlier. We take a picture of ourselves there and roam onward, stopping at a stand to buy candy. Rivia tells me which ones are her favorites. Some of them I recognize; others I don't. Later in the evening, we go out for a nice dinner, and then go to bed.

Tired and with a thousand new impressions and feelings, I lie down in my hotel bed and have a hard time falling asleep. The sounds of the city and the traffic outside come right through the walls. It hits me as I lie there that my home in Umeå is quiet and comfortable. Maybe the snowplow comes through once during the night. But here, there's always someone awake.

My Best Friend Saves My Life
São Paulo, 1980s

I don't remember the whole thing. I just remember that Camile and I
had decided to sleep in one of the nicer neighborhoods that bordered
on the poorer part of the city. The day had been a day like all the others, which meant a constant struggle to find food. We had run around
on the streets, begging for money, and had stolen wallets and all sorts
of things from people's pockets. Every now and then, someone would
notice us, and all we could do was run as fast as we could. We had
various hiding spots prepared, and there was always a rendezvous point
where we would find each other if we got separated. And we always had
a strategy, like when we were picking pockets: If the person notices you
but doesn't manage to grab you—run! In the rare event that the person
grabs your arm and has a hold on you—bite them on the hand or kick
them in the shin! Once you get free—*run* for your life! The person you
hurt will be really mad. If someone does nab you and you're totally
trapped, there's not much you can do. Just try to hit as hard as you can,
kick, bite, scratch. If it's a man, try to kick him between the legs. If you
do manage to get free—run like you've never run before!

There was one more alternative when you got caught, and that was
when there were two or more of you working together. The others could

step in and distract the person while you got free and then, yet again, you would run for your life.

Our day had consisted of the usual, nothing special. We fought together, and we laughed together. As usual, like sisters, we split everything we managed to get, and we tried to steer clear of grown-ups, street kids who were older than us, and anyone in a gang. But even if a gang consisted of children younger than us, both Camile and I had learned the hard way that if there were enough of them, they could easily hurt us. We stood no chance against ten determined kids all working together, kids who had learned to kick, scratch, and bite. So, we steered clear.

As street kids, it wasn't hard to remain invisible. Most people pretended they didn't see us. The only time they actually saw us was when we were standing right in front of them and begging, when we tugged on their clothes and asked as nicely as we could for change to get some food: "Please, sir, could you spare any change for some food? I haven't eaten in several days." Or, "Please, beautiful lady, we're hungry children." It rarely worked. But we called out kind words to anyone who did give us a bit of money, saying that we hoped a saint would preserve them or something like that. To those who didn't give us anything, who pushed us away, or hit us, we screamed a litany of curse words. We used the very worst words we knew, and believe me, we knew a lot.

That was what we did every day. And just about every day, people called us rats. Every time they did, we tuned them out and pretended not to hear. I don't know what was worse, being spit on and pushed away, or being totally ignored. If someone spit on us, at least they saw us, and that was confirmation of our existence. Being totally ignored was like not existing at all, as if you weren't a human among other humans.

There were those who didn't give us any money but still took the time to see us, say hi, give us a nice smile. That took the chill off. We street children rarely received love from outside, but we gave one another warmth—we danced and laughed—because despite everything, we were kids, and we longed for the opportunity to play and laugh from the heart.

Rarely in Sweden have I felt that same true, genuine, wonderful laughter bubbling up inside me. In Brazil, the raw intensity of my feelings, the pain and the joy, was so much greater. When I was happy as a child in Brazil, my sense of joy was so much stronger and could be elicited by little things, like getting to eat a real meal or ice cream. And the pain . . . it could feel bottomless.

We'd come into the nicer neighborhood, when we saw a man standing outside a shop. Camile pretended to bump into him, and he chewed her out. She stood nicely and took the scolding. He told her to keep her eyes open and pay attention to what was going on around her. Camile played a little shy and modest and said she was so terribly sorry. Meanwhile, I plunged my hand into his right back pocket and stole his wallet. The man went into the shop. When he got up to the cash register and reached to take out his wallet, at first he looked confused. His hands started searching in all his pockets. Then he realized his wallet was gone. He looked irritated at first, then angry.

Camile and I were standing outside the window, looking in. He was the one who should keep his eyes open! We laughed until our bellies ached. As soon as he saw us, we ran as hard as we could away from there. When we felt like we were far enough away that we wouldn't be caught, we sat down on a bench and opened the wallet. There were a few bills and coins. We took them and discarded the wallet. We went into a restaurant and bought two big skewers of meat that had been dipped in this amazingly good sauce. I had never tasted anything so good.

We had a little money left over, so we each bought an icepop from a nice man. He had a white pushcart with two big narrow wheels in the front and two long sticks for handles at the back that allowed him to roll his cart where he wanted. The icepops were super tasty and cold, which was great, because it had been an unbelievably hot day. I bought a pinkish-orangish one, and Camile bought a yellow one. Hers tasted like mango and mine, papaya. Of course, I thought hers tasted better than mine; she laughed at me and traded hers for mine. The icepops were cylindrical. Someone had poured juice into plastic tubes, and it was like sucking on frozen water that tasted like juice. If you sucked super hard on it, the color would disappear from the part of the ice you'd sucked on, and only a section of white crystalline ice would remain, which tasted like water. But it was so good. We played and had a great time. Toward the end of the day, we were both exhausted from all the fun we'd had, from the heat, and from having run so much. Maybe that was one reason one of us didn't manage to get away.

I have been so mad at Camile for not running faster, for not being speedier. I know it doesn't make sense to be mad at her for that. What happened certainly wasn't her fault or mine, but I was the one who ran faster, and I was the one who survived.

As our day wound down and night approached, it was time for Camile and me to find someplace to sleep. We knew the risk of sleeping in the nicer neighborhoods, but we took it since things were really rough in the favela right then, more so than usual. Sometimes we wandered into the nicer neighborhoods at nighttime, never that far in, but far enough to be able to spy on the rich people through their windows. We would climb over walls and fences, and one time we were chased by two big dogs. Camile and I just barely managed to climb over a metal fence with barbed wire. I could feel the breath from one of the dogs on my bare foot, and my foot was spared by only a few inches.

One night, Camile and I crawled on our knees up to a beautiful white house and peeked in a window. We saw a room that took our breath away. It was a pink room overflowing with dolls and toys. The room had a white bed, and the bed was covered with stuffed animals. A girl, a white girl, was lying in the bed, sleeping. She looked so peaceful there, and jealousy and longing welled up in me. A lamp was on next to her bed, and the door to her room was ajar.

This night, however, when we ran for our lives, wasn't one of those when Camile and I were curious enough about rich people to peek in their windows. Although we did decide to sleep where we didn't really belong. It was a warm night, so warm that we didn't hold each other the way we usually did. I can't say what time it was, because I didn't have a watch; even if I had had one, I wouldn't have known how to read it.

Our days usually consisted of the same routine. It got light out, you woke up with your tummy rumbling, and then the shops opened. Some people were walking around, others were driving cars, some were on their way to work, others didn't know where they were going. In the slum, there were always some women standing around doing laundry, some children running around, a few tough guys strutting by, some babies crying, someone laughing, and someone sitting in the sun, leaning against their shack. Makeshift fireplaces emitted smoke, and you could smell the scent of spices in the air. Colorful clothes hung drying on lines here and there, and soccer balls were always whizzing by. There were tons of children, children everywhere. Sometimes it felt like there were only children and no adults. Later in the day, bellies grew hungry again, and people moved a little slower, a little more tiredly. Night came and it got dark, and people lay down to sleep wherever they found a spot, where they hoped they'd be relatively safe. In the nicer neighborhoods, there would be fewer people on the move, but we didn't belong there.

I don't know how long Camile and I had been asleep when I woke up with a bad feeling in the pit of my stomach. I had heard something. I gave Camile a little nudge to wake her up. She looked at me, and I moved my finger to my lips to tell her to be quiet. She understood right away and sat up. I pointed to my ear to indicate to her that I'd heard something, and then I pointed to the corner of the building. Camile looked worried and tense. I think my fear had worn off on her.

We looked at each other and tried to make sense of what I'd heard. It didn't take long before we heard voices. There were some men talking. We didn't hear that much of their conversation, but the way they were talking—their tone and hard laughter—told us all we needed to know. We needed to get out of there, and fast. It was highly likely that the men were clearing the neighborhood of "rats."

Camile and I peeked around the corner to see how our chances looked. We saw kids standing in a row. And the instant our little heads appeared around the corner, one of the men spotted us.

"Looky there! We've got a few more. Run over there and get 'em!" said the man who'd spotted us.

"Run, Christiana, run!" I heard Camile yell to me.

"Get 'em!" was the last thing I heard before we were running full out, as hard as we could.

Camile kept yelling for me to run. I was scared and ran for my life. The terror and panic in Camile's voice scared me even more, and it was hard to think straight. Fear had almost completely taken over. I cast one last glance backward and saw that Camile had wound up a little behind me. I slowed down so she could catch up, but when she noticed, she yelled at me to run faster, to keep running. I yelled back that she had to run faster. I picked up my pace again, and I saw the men getting closer and closer to Camile. There was sheer terror in her eyes. I had no idea where I was running. I came to a low wall and jumped up so my hands got a firm hold on the top edge of the wall. As I pulled myself up with my hands, I scrabbled up with my bare feet. It vaguely registered with me that both my arms and legs were getting scraped, but I couldn't feel it. Quick as a flash, I got up onto the wall and turned around to hold my hand down for Camile. She wasn't far behind. I saw her running toward me, and I saw that the two men were gaining on her. I screamed for her to run faster, and I saw the panic in her eyes when she realized she wasn't going to make it. The men nabbed her, and Camile screamed and writhed, struggling to get free.

I was about to jump back down and help her, the way we always did, when she yelled for me to run.

One of the men came at me, and I didn't know what to do. Camile yelled again, "Run!"

Without thinking, without having actively made any decision, I turned and ran. I heard the man who was holding Camile yell to the other man, "To hell with her." I ran and kept running until my brain had calmed down a little and I could start to think again.

I discovered that I wasn't being chased anymore and stopped. My heart was pounding hard. It felt like it was in my mouth and not in my chest. I was gasping for breath, and my feet were killing me. I looked down at my legs and saw that my shins and knees were covered with scrapes, but I couldn't feel any pain. What should I do? I had to get back to Camile. I had to help her! I slowly started making my way back between the buildings, trying to remember which way I'd run, so I could try to take a different route back. Eventually I heard some children crying plaintively. I heard the men talking again, and knew I was close. A terrible, nasty sense of nausea rose from my stomach. I took a deep breath and carefully peeked around the corner. Five or six children stood lined up. A dark van was parked near them, and there were three men. I remember that I saw an older boy, around ten or twelve years old, holding a little girl's hand. They both looked terrified. The girl was crying. Camile was standing next to the girl. She looked scared, too. She kept looking around, as if searching for something, someone. She looked so small and frightened.

I had never thought of Camile as small or fearful. She was Camile—cleverer than I was at everything, smarter, and better all around. It was weird to see her looking so vulnerable, so little. It hit me that what she kept looking around for was me. She was waiting for me to help her.

The men stood with their backs to me, and I dared to peek out a little farther. Camile turned her head my way, and our eyes met. I didn't know what to do, so I started looking around to see whether I could find anything that might help. What, I didn't know. If I jumped one of the men, maybe the rest of the kids could take the other two men down? But the men were armed, and I'd never be able to take down one of the men on my own. It would take at least five to ten kids to take one of those men out of commission. I was starting to panic again. I looked at Camile. I'm sure she understood what I was thinking, because she slowly and cautiously shook her head as her eyes said, *Don't do anything stupid*.

The men moved away from the children a little. Some of the kids cried; some screamed. Camile just stood there, her eyes incredibly sad and frightened, but there was something about the look in her eyes. Maybe I was too young then to put words to what it was, but there was no mistaking the emotion. She smiled a slight smile that was for me, and then I remember everything clearly and in slow motion. I watched how something strange happened to her forehead. I remember that as her body fell to the ground in the most bizarre way, my right hand flew up and covered my mouth, and my scream stuck in my throat. The last thing I heard was the gunshot. It felt like an eternity before Camile's body hit the ground. As I looked at my friend's lifeless body lying about eighty feet in front of me, I heard more gunshots. Instinctively I turned and started running.

I ran. I ran as hard as I could. I ran so my feet, knees, and lungs ached. I cried. I cried so much. The tears stopped me from seeing where I was going, but my body kept moving, turning left and then right, proceeding straight ahead. During this possessed and rapid flight, I saw Camile's body collapsing. I saw her face. I saw her smile. I saw how she took a deep breath, and before she had time to exhale, I saw her body collapse. I ran into someone. I ran into something. I heard someone yelling at me in irritation. I just ran, ran far away from the men, from Camile's body, from everything. My body had taken over. I was on autopilot. I couldn't think what to do, didn't know where I was going. All I saw was Camile, collapsing to the ground again and again.

When I woke up, I was lying in a fetal position with my knees under my chin. I rolled over to put my arms around Camile, but she wasn't there. The image of how she had smiled at me sadly popped into my head, and I broke down. I was alone, and I cried like I'd never cried before. I was under our concrete staircase, and I was completely alone. I would never see Camile again. She would never hold me under our stairs. I would never again hear her beautiful voice and her amazing stories. What was I going to do? I didn't want to live without her. The pain was so visceral and cut deep into my gut. I couldn't breathe. It was as if I suddenly didn't know how to breathe. There was something wrong with my heart. It hurt. It felt like a thousand knives were piercing me, and then everything went black . . .

I don't know how long it was black. I only know that when I woke up, I was lying next to vomit, my vomit. My eyes stung. I didn't move. I didn't care. I lay there, and I saw her smile at me again and again and saw how something happened to her forehead and she collapsed. I knew that life would be much darker without Camile. *Please, come back. Please come back!*

I knew that she wouldn't come back. I lay under the stairs for a long time. I remember that it got light, and I remember that it got dark. I remember that I noticed that several times. When I woke up from my fog, I was changed. Something was different. The world was darker. I was darker. Part of my soul died with Camile, and I understood what those thousand knives I'd felt were: it was a part of me dying. I sat up and hugged my knees. I looked at the pile of vomit in front of me. I was tired, so tired. I perceived no hunger, no joy, and no sorrow. I was an empty husk that just sat there. And I planned to sit there for a long time, until I died or until Camile came back.

Mamãe used to tell me that if my heart ever hurt too much, I should sleep, and when I woke up, everything would feel a lot better. I wondered whether death was like that. You fell asleep and then woke up somewhere in the sky, and everything felt much better.

Camile never came back, but my mother did. She found me under the stairs where she knew we sometimes slept, Camile and I. Mamãe came. She stroked my hair, she hugged me, and she whispered away my nightmares. Everything got a little better, and then even a little better still. It's incredible what a parent's love can do. Without my mother's presence, I'm sure I would never have moved beyond the numb stage. I probably would have become a ghost, and incredibly vulnerable on the streets.

Mamãe kissed my forehead and my cheeks and cried with me.

"Christiana, life is terrible and unfair sometimes, but never stop walking. Always keep walking," she told me. I remember wondering why. "Because after everything that's happened to us, our hearts want what's good, and our hearts can't be the only things that want that. You're not alone, because there are people who see you and watch over you. Do you understand?"

No, I didn't. Who'd seen Camile? Who'd watched over her? It wasn't fair, and I refused to understand it.

"One day you will, and until then, promise me you'll always keep walking. No matter how much it hurts, you keep walking!"

"Where should I walk, Mamãe?"

"It doesn't matter. Just make sure that you never stop walking, OK?" She stood up and held out her hand to me. I put my hand in hers, and we walked.

Up There in the Clouds
2015

It may not come as a surprise that later in my life I chose to do track and field. I ran the two-hundred-, four-hundred-, and eight-hundred-meter events. My specialty was four hundred meters. After all, I'd gotten a good foundation in this as a kid. Running was something I could do. Running was something I did most of the time. I was really fast. Unfortunately, my track and field career ended after an operation on my right foot. When I was nineteen, the doctors said my feet were shot. I had the feet of a fifty-year-old.

I've always been physically active, ever since I was little. I always want to be in motion, and I love climbing and running. Sports have satisfied that drive in me and become a relief valve to let off pressure.

As I stand in my hotel room now, looking out over the city of São Paulo, which spreads out below me, I wonder if you could do a base jump from this balcony.

A little more than twenty years ago, I had a dream of sitting in the clouds, a dream about flying. And in 2011, I went to the Umeå Skydiving Club's homepage and signed up for a class. When I told my friends that I was going to try skydiving, several of them wondered what was wrong with me. But I never had an instant's doubt that I would love flying. Sure, it would be nerve-wracking and difficult to take the plunge and hurl myself out of an airplane, but that anxiety was probably just a sign of being a healthy person.

Six guys and I took the class together in Umeå. Once we were done with the theoretical component, it was time to make the jump, unwind our wings (parachutes), and hope for a soft landing. We got into the cars and drove down to Söderhamn where we, seven excited and somewhat nervous people, would make our first jump. I remember it as if it were yesterday, and I'll never forget it.

Skydiving is a weather-dependent sport. The wind can't be too strong, the clouds can't be too low, and it's better if it's not raining.

This weekend it was partially cloudy with some occasional rain showers. The instructors were there to help us and the other would-be jumpers who were also trying to earn their certification. The instructors drew straws to see who would get to jump first so it would be fair. I, who obviously wanted to be one of the first to jump, wound up being one of the last. I didn't want to have too much time to think. I'd just get nervous. I didn't want to sit and watch while everyone else jumped. Once you've decided to jump, you simply want to get it over with. That's just how it is.

The first day went by, and I sat and watched as student after student got to go up and jump. They came down. Some waxed lyrical; others were pale in the face. I sat there the whole day and didn't get to jump. My nervousness kept increasing, and by the next day, I was all wound up. I sat on the ground and ran through the jump in my mind. I would be jumping out of an AN-28 airplane. It had a rear ramp, which meant that my two instructors and I would jump out of the back of the plane standing up. In the air, I would arch my back and maintain a stable falling position. I would jump out at a height of thirteen thousand feet, and when I got down to five thousand feet, I would wave my hands in front of my face to show the instructors that I was planning to pull my parachute. Then, while holding my left hand in front of my face to maintain balance, I would bring my right hand back to grab the hacky (the little ball on the right side of the gear) and open my parachute.

I know that muscle memory is important, so I put on my gear, the parachute, and lie down on the ground on my stomach and arch my back. I watch my left hand where the altimeter will be. I pretend it shows five thousand feet, wave, and then bring my right hand to the ball and pretend to pull my chute. I repeat this several times. Each time, my hand finds the little ball right away, and I feel confident. There won't be any problems. I'll be able to open my chute. My two instructors come over to me. They make sure I've put my equipment on correctly, and they check my reserve chute. Jens, my primary instructor, asks me to run through the jump. I describe to him in detail what I'm planning to do in the air. Both instructors seem satisfied. After that, all the skydivers start boarding the plane, and I'm one of them. My nervousness kicks into overdrive, my sweat glands activate, and my pulse speeds up.

I try to appear cool, but the looks of encouragement the other skydivers give me tell me that my nervousness is showing. There are twenty-four of us in the plane. The engine starts, and the plane begins taxiing. My heart pounds a little harder, a little faster. I make eye contact with Jens, and he gives me a reassuring smile. The plane lifts off, and there's no turning back now. In fifteen minutes—the time it takes for the plane to reach thirteen thousand feet—I will fling myself out of a fully functioning aircraft. *Am I an idiot? What was I thinking?*

I take a few deep breaths, remind myself why I'm doing this, remind myself of what I believe I can accomplish by going through with this dive. And somewhere in the middle of all this, I close my eyes and picture my legs—next to Mamãe's—dangling over the edge of the cave. I remember how strong the longing to fly was in me even as a child. And I hear Mamãe telling me that nothing is impossible.

I open my eyes and look at the other skydivers sitting in front of me—if they can do it, so can I. We're at an altitude of about eight thousand feet now, and Jens turns to me and asks me to run through the jump one more time. I focus on him and take myself through the jump again. After that, we put on our goggles, and suddenly the whole thing is very real. I see how the other jumpers are laughing and putting on their helmets, gloves, and goggles. They look so relaxed. I hear the pilot's voice on the speaker. The rear ramp opens. Cold air rushes in. I'm sitting fairly far back in the plane but can still see parts of the sky through the hole in the back there. My pulse is crazy fast now. I hear the pilot's voice: "Green light, green light, jump, jump!" *What?* I think . . . *Are we supposed to jump now? But I don't know if I'm ready . . .*

The skydivers start hurling themselves out of the plane. My instructor and I have taken up our positions, and I feel my legs shaking something awful. I follow the flow and watch as jumpers dive out of the plane. I approach the opening, thinking that maybe I don't want to do this after all. I look back and see the others pushing forward. I have no choice. I find myself looking into a guy's eyes, and I see my own nervousness reflected in the look on his face. We've reached the ramp now. I turn around and back out to the edge. I try to force the feeling of panic out of my head and focus on what I need to do. I look at Jens, he looks and me, and I nod. He nods back. I repeat the same procedure with my other instructor, Magnus, who's standing on my other side. I bend my trembling legs and shout, very quickly, the line that I had repeated so many times calmly and slowly down on the ground: "Ready, set, *go!*"

And then I step out of the plane, out into the air.

On the way out, one of my instructors happens to bump into the plane, and I catch the wind wrong. Instead of landing on a soft cushion of air, I start tumbling. I tumble around and around. One minute, I see the ground; the next, I see the plane and the sky. I remember filling up with joy, thinking, *This is how it feels to fly*. I smile and completely forget that I have a protocol to follow. I feel my instructor Magnus let go of me, and I start coming back to reality. I remember hearing about situations that would cause the instructor to let go. *Wait a second,* I think . . . *That means things aren't going that well for me . . .* I turn my head and see that Jens has a firm hold on my right arm and my right leg. We're still tumbling, and I understand that he's trying to correct the situation and stabilize my fall. I know it's dangerous to open your parachute if you're not falling stably. You can get tangled up. I immediately return to reality and arch my back with all my might while gently bending my legs and reaching my arms forward in a semicircle. It takes less than a second before I'm in a stable falling position. I look at my altimeter and see that it shows eleven thousand feet. I've tumbled for sixteen hundred feet.

I start the protocol. I look down at the ground, see only a green mass, but choose a meadow on the horizon as my *heading* (a point I will look at to keep from losing my orientation). When I'm at five thousand feet, I wave my hands in front of my face and leave the left one there while bringing the right one back to grab the little ball. I don't find it. I try again but can't find it. I've practiced this hundreds of times. It should be there . . . But I can't find it. I feel the panic setting in. *Where the hell is the ball?* I need to be able to pull my ripcord.

Suddenly, I feel a yank. I look up and watch as my red parachute catches the air, cell by cell, until it unfurls fully. I realize that Jens must have pulled my ripcord for me. It's the instructor's job to make sure the students' parachutes open if they initially fail. But it's not over yet. I'm hanging under a parachute three thousand feet above the earth now. And I don't have any instructors to help me. I look around to see if there are any other parachutes near me. I grab both steering handles to the brake lines and try to see where I'm going to land. I feel panicky. This is the part that's worried me the most, being on my own for the landing. I grow increasingly nervous when I can't locate the drop zone. I start wondering if I'm even facing into the wind properly. Am I flying toward the drop zone or away from it? I peek down at the ground to see whether I can tell which way the wind is blowing, but the ground is just green. Then it occurs to me that I'm supposed to have my back to the sun, which is to my left. If I do that, then I'll be flying in the right direction. Finally, I see the landing field. I brake the parachute and land gently and neatly on the grass.

The landing feels as smooth as stepping off a curb. I did it! I threw myself out of a plane at an altitude of thirteen thousand feet. I fell at one hundred twenty-four miles per hour, sailed with my parachute, and landed beautifully near the other jumpers. I'm so happy, so proud. And for the first time in as long as I can remember, I feel like I'm free.

I probably won't earn the certification, since I didn't open my own chute. Still, I feel only joy.

People have told me many times that I must have a death wish to engage in such a dangerous sport, or that I must be an "adrenaline junkie." But it's not like that for me. I have fought to live for my whole life. I skydive because I feel free when I'm doing it and because it's so beautiful up there among the clouds. My brain has to focus 100 percent on being in the present. That means that for the sixty seconds a free fall takes, before my parachute opens, I can't think about what was or what will be. There aren't very many other occasions in life when I've succeeded in finding moments like that, where I can just exist in the present.

Adrenaline was coursing through my blood as I gathered up my chute and wandered toward my jump mates. Everyone asked how it had gone. I just laughed and said that I thought I probably flunked. Then Jens came over to me and asked me to review the jump. I told him everything I remembered. When I was done, he looked kind of surprised and told me it was unusual to have such detailed memories from a first jump. I remember thinking that this wasn't the first time my brain had had to operate in a life-or-death situation. And I passed on my first jump.

Only a small number of Swedes are involved in this extreme sport, and I'm one of them. About fifteen hundred of us are licensed, and only 20 percent of us are women. I've wondered what we have in common, we women who jump. Aside from our shared love of the sport, we're all different, with different backgrounds, personalities, ages, and social classes. I assume that these other women have their own reasons for taking up skydiving. For me, it started when I was a kid on the other side of the Atlantic Ocean, sitting atop my little cave. A few words from my mother that I have followed my entire life: "Nothing is impossible." I have tried to live by them. And fears are there to be conquered. I could have made my dream of flight a reality as soon as I turned eighteen, but it took me ten years to unfurl my wings. I believe that everything comes when we're ready, and once we've opened a door, it can be hard to shut again. I pretty much always berate myself when I don't succeed or don't do something well enough. And even when I thought I had failed at what I had dreamed of doing for so long, I felt nothing but happiness, total freedom.

I've continued skydiving. Every cloud I pass through, I feel that Mamãe and Camile are with me. Maybe I don't bounce from cloud to cloud, the way I thought I would when I was little, but I fall through them with joy. I still grin with delight every time I jump. The first time I fell through a cloud, one of my instructors, Gunlög, laughed at me because I tried to shield my face. Even though I knew clouds weren't solid matter, my childhood fantasy that you could walk from cloud to cloud was deeply rooted in me, so deeply that more than twenty years later, I tried to shield my face from hitting something hard when I encountered clouds. Gunlög laughed at me even more when I did the same thing the next time.

The Story of the Cloud People
São Paulo, late 1980s

When I skydive, I often think of Camile. She told me a story once, and it's imprinted on me. I even wrote it down when I was little because it made such a strong impression. Maybe I remember it so well because it was the last story Camile told me before I lost her.

Camile and I were sitting on some cardboard under a concrete staircase. It was night, and it was dark and cozy where we were, outside some factory that manufactured something, though what, we had no idea. I had always liked the dark, especially when Mamãe and I lived in the woods. There was something warm and safe about being surrounded by darkness. Out in the woods, you could see all the stars and the fireflies. There had been a time when I believed that the stars were fireflies that had flown too high and gotten stuck on black flypaper. I knew better now, since Mamãe had told me that fireflies couldn't fly that high and that the stars I saw were big, burning fireballs, which looked small to us because they were so far away. I also knew that the darkness, however much I liked it, contained evil as well. Things happened at night that didn't happen during the day. The darkness hid the evil, and when the light returned, it was as if the darkness had never existed.

Camile and I were sharing an orange, a piece of bread, and two half-eaten sausages that I'd found in a dumpster behind a restaurant. We shared everything equally.

"Tell me a story," I said to her, my mouth full of bread. Camile would tell these fabulous stories about strange animals, evil people, and different worlds, stories that always ended happily.

"OK."

We sat in silence for a bit, and I knew that she was thinking about what story to tell. I was impatient, as I usually was, but I knew that if I wanted to hear a story, it was best to keep quiet and wait. A few minutes elapsed, and it felt like an eternity. But in the end, she started to tell the story, and I settled in and pricked up my ears. Camile's voice sounded like a soft whisper as she began: "In a world above the ground, somewhere between the earth and the sky, lived the cloud people."

I smiled because I loved everything that had to do with clouds, and Camile knew it. Here is the story she told me:

The Cloud People

by Camile

In a world above the ground, somewhere between the earth and the sky, lived the cloud people. What you need to know about the cloud people is that they were all good. They did not discriminate based on skin color, since they themselves were made up of all the colors of the rainbow, and they called themselves the Colored Ones. Hatred and pain did not exist in their world, but tears did. This was how they could still distinguish the good from the bad that people did to one another. When they saw someone do something terrible, it made them so sad that they cried. When they saw someone do something nice, they all came together and held hands, and they formed the most beautiful thing they could—a rainbow.

One day, two of the cloud people's sons climbed down to the earth. One was yellow and the other was blue. Their assignment was to study the humans. The yellow one was going to investigate the good side, whereas the blue one's assignment was to investigate the bad side. The yellow one was sent to the people in the forest, an Indian tribe who lived in harmony with the woods and the animals. The blue one was sent to the city of São Paulo, where he would live with a street gang. The Indians helped the yellow one find their little hamlet, and they took care of him, fed him, gave him a little shack to sleep in, and told him he was welcome to stay for as long as he wanted. The yellow one lived there happily and experienced all the joy these humans had to give. And this caused him to begin to glow. Around his head, he really shone. The chieftain asked who he was, and the yellow one told about his people and the purpose of his visit. The chieftain asked if his tribe had disappointed him, and the yellow one replied, "We only shine when we're surrounded by joy and love." The yellow one thanked the Indians and rejoined his own people, but before he disappeared, a luminous rainbow, brighter than ever before, shone over the Indians.

The blue one went looking for the bad people in São Paulo. He intended to make the hearts of the wicked shine with love again. He found a gang and watched them. The more bad deeds the gang perpetrated, the more he despaired. He realized that to get close to them, they would require him to do something abominable. One day, the leader told the blue one that if he killed a little boy who had stolen something, he could join their gang. The blue one felt something bad growing inside him with every day he remained on earth. One day, he went up to the little boy and killed him. Then he sat down and cried. He cried all night long. It was as if something inside him had died, as if a light had been extinguished. Finally, the day came when he was supposed to return home. When he got home, he saw that everyone was staring at him with contempt. They were so disgusted at him for what he'd done that as punishment, they trapped him in a cloud and stationed ten guards to keep him there. He started to hate, and with every day that passed, his hatred grew even stronger until there was nothing left in his heart but hate. He spread darkness to the guards' hearts and managed to convince them to let him out. The cloud was now so filled with hate that fire came out of it. Finally, the Colored Ones recognized the danger and were forced to learn to protect themselves. Even today, an unending battle is going on between the Colored Ones and the evil cloud people.

"That's why we see both light and dark clouds in the sky," Camile said. And with that, yet another wonderful story came to an end.

"Camile?" I asked.

"Hmm," she replied, as if ready for me to start peppering her with a hundred questions.

"It must be weird not to have a name, to just be called the yellow one or the blue one. How would anyone know who anyone is? How would you know who I am? How would I call to you if I lost you?"

Camile smiled and then answered me with another question: "Why would you lose me?"

"Because maybe we got separated."

"Christiana, do you think the Indians forgot the yellow one?"

"No!"

"Well then, they haven't lost him, have they? And that's why we'll never lose each other."

Camile was a miniature copy of my mother, and sometimes it annoyed me that she was smarter than I was. She wasn't that much older. She was like a wise little old lady, an old soul. She would give me a ton of riddles that often took me way too long to figure out, and I would just feel dumb.

"Are you and I the yellow one and the blue one?" I asked her.

"Why do you think that?"

"Because you usually tell stories that are about two people, and it feels like you're talking about us."

"No, this wasn't about us. If it had been about us, we'd have both been yellow." She smiled and took my hand. And that night we slept as we often did, on top of flattened cardboard boxes, our arms around each other.

When I think about Camile now, I realize that it's not a coincidence that I like fantasy books. I read them to feel Camile's presence and to sink into a world of magic where anything is possible, but also because the stories make you think about life and people. Patrick Rothfuss's fantasy book *The Name of the Wind* is on my hotel-room nightstand. When I think back to what happened to Camile and to the bottomless pit I fell into even as a child, his words comfort me. He says that we have an unparalleled ability to face pain and that we can do it by going through four different stages. The first is the sleep that gives us protection and distance. The second is forgetting, because some wounds are too deep to heal. The third is madness: when reality is only pain, you must escape it. The fourth is death. Nothing can harm us after death.

I know exactly what it means to go through the first three stages that Patrick Rothfuss describes. I have no experience with the last stage, but there have been times when the pain was so great that death didn't feel so far off.

When I look out at this concrete city now, where for a part of my life I experienced pain and grief, joy and friendship, it comforts me to think that if I talk about our time together, Camile doesn't just live on in me. Instead, she lives forever. While so many children disappear, die, and are forgotten, her name will live on, and a part of her story will live on through me and my tale. I know that she would have wanted the truth to come out. And the truth was that the military police, the ones who were supposed to protect the people, cleansed the neighborhoods of street children. Hearing about it today, you might think it sounds like a wicked fairy tale. Unfortunately, it was real. And unfortunately, it's still happening.

For a long time, I was ashamed that I hadn't been brave enough to step out around that corner, where I had hidden. I regretted not going to Camile and holding her hand and accompanying her on what would have been our last journey. Sadly, our biggest regrets are also the ones that follow us the rest of our lives. I know it's irrational. There was no point to Camile's death, and there wouldn't have been to mine, either. But you just don't abandon your friend and sister. And yet that was exactly what I did. The absurd thing is that for so many years, I've felt bad and blamed myself for someone else's evil deed. It makes me mad, but above all unbelievably miserable, that at the age of six or seven, I was put in a situation where I was forced to choose between dying with my friend or living with the consequences of not doing so.

We can put all sorts of different labels on what we do and who we are, but they're just words, and words aren't actions. Our actions are what define us. There's a saying that if you love someone, you should set them free, and if you're lucky, they'll find their way back to you. I contend that the same approach works for hate; when you let go of hate, you set yourself free. Hate consumes you. For so many years, I hated those men for what they did to my best friend and to me. They took Camile's life, and they took a piece of mine. They're not worth any more of me, of my life.

Children Give Words Wings

Camile meant and continues to mean so much to me, even today. We shared adventures and painful experiences during our childhood. I will remember her and our time together with joy, laughter, and warmth. She was a clever little girl who had a gift for storytelling, and she gave so much warmth and happiness to those who knew her. So instead of only remembering the dark and terrible, I also carry this memory of Camile with me:

One day, Camile looked at me, picked up a pebble, and threw it at me.

"What are you sitting around moping about now?" she asked provocatively.

"I'm wondering why it's so hard to understand the words grown-ups say. Why do they always seem to understand one another, but sometimes it's hard for me to understand them? Am I dumb?"

"You're a little dumb," she teased me with a grin. "But I think what you mean is that it's not their words, but what they're trying to say that is hard to understand."

"That's what I just said!"

"No, Christiana, you said their *words* were hard. Those are two different things."

"That is, too, what I said!"

"Now you're being dumb!"

"No, you're being dumb!" I snapped back, and stuck my tongue out at her. She rolled her eyes. I picked up the same pebble she'd thrown at me and threw it back at her. Camile started laughing. We were both sitting cross-legged on the ground. We weren't sitting far from each other and were playing in the red dirt, building little houses and trying to shape small mud animals. Camile kept laughing, and I told her that wasn't cool. I could tell she was trying hard to stop laughing, but that just made her laugh even harder. I tried to look mad, but it got more and more difficult not to be caught up in her contagious laugh. In the end, we were both writhing with laughter.

When Camile finally stopped laughing, she said, "God gave us words."

She gesticulated with both hands, making a big circle to show how monumental this was.

"Grown-ups try to understand them"—she pointed to her head with her right pointer finger—"but we children are the ones who give them wings."

She flapped her arms as if she were a chicken.

"And we make the words fly."

She stood up and held out her hand to me.

I took it and got up. She started running, her arms stretched out like the wings of an airplane. She tilted her body to the right and then to the left, and I followed her and did the same thing. We were both laughing, and she looked back at me and smiled a huge grin. And then she ran right into a signpost and fell on her butt.

I stopped. I was a little shocked at first, but when I saw that she was OK, I started laughing at her. She gave me a grumpy look, and I managed to get out a few words between laughing fits. "Apparently, God thinks you should be down on the ground; otherwise he probably wouldn't have knocked you down so hard."

Camile stuck her tongue out at me, and I kept on laughing. Then she laughed.

That's the kind of person she was.

The Favela

São Paulo, 1989–1991

Mamãe had taught me how to make a slingshot when we lived in the caves, what to consider when you picked the wood and rubber to achieve a stable, accurate, good slingshot. Santos already had a slingshot, and I taught Camile how to make one and tried to teach her how to aim to hit her prey, which in the favela was usually other kids, animals, or just something on the street.

I don't know whether it was a failure in my teaching or whether Camile just had no aptitude when it came to the slingshot, but she was a shockingly bad shot. One time when she was aiming at a bottle, she managed to shoot the stone 180 degrees in the other direction, hitting herself in the eye. To this day, I still haven't figured out how she did that.

Santos and I always had our slingshots stuffed into the back pockets of our shorts. We used to take them out and play with them when Camile wasn't around. That way, no children would be at risk of going blind.

Camile and Santos asked me one day if I knew how to make a kite. I had watched my mother do it, but had never learned how. We gathered the parts to make the kite: Santos got some bamboo, Camile got string, and I ran off to look for plastic garbage bags. Once we'd found everything, we sat down and got to work. Santos's job was to make two thin sticks out of the bamboo stalk he was holding. They couldn't be too heavy because then the kite wouldn't take off and fly. And they couldn't be too thin because they might snap in two. Camile was untangling the loose string she'd found. She looped the end and carefully wound it around the middle of a plastic bottle so it wouldn't get tangled. I ripped little rectangular pieces off the plastic bags. When we were done with the preparations, we started to assemble our kite. Santos, who had made two nice bamboo sticks, started attaching one of the bags I'd found. Camile and I tied the rectangular bits of plastic to three long strings, which would form the kite's tails. Then we tied the tails to the kite and secured the string, which Camile had so neatly wound around the plastic bottle, to the middle of the kite where the sticks crossed. Santos took hold of the kite and held it up proudly to the sky while Camile and I did a happy dance. It was time to fly our kite. Santos was up first. With the kite in one hand and the empty bottle with the string in the other, he started running. Camile and I ran barefoot alongside him while we watched the kite catch the wind and rise into the sky. I remember thinking that I wanted to be a kite so I could fly, too.

The Ill-Fated Fight

The boy died. It was my fault. I know I didn't mean for it to happen, but I still have to live with what I did for the rest of my life.

Many nights I have woken up in a cold sweat, seeing his shocked, stunned eyes staring into my own. It's an unbelievably awful feeling, one that eats away at me, carrying the knowledge that I've extinguished another person's life, a person who lived under the same conditions I did. I see that same look every time I wake up from my nightmares and have the same feeling: if I never achieve happiness in this life, it's because I don't deserve to.

People say that the strongest survive, but I wonder if it isn't the most desperate. I've never been as hungry and in such a weakened state as I was then. I think desperation was the biggest reason things turned out so badly. I had lost both Santos and Camile, my best friends, and my mother and I had had to endure so much. I couldn't take another injustice, even if it came from someone who had also been treated unfairly. Nothing anyone can say to me can make me feel any sorrier or worse than I've felt all these years. To get up every morning and look at myself in the mirror and try to ignore everything I see there isn't easy. It's there, it's a part of me, and there's no way to run from it. In a way, I don't want to, either; that would be too easy. I could never have imagined that the human body was so weak, so frail, that someone who breathes, talks, smiles, runs, and exists right here in the present, can so easily be taken away, that something we take for granted can vanish so easily. This may be hard for a grown-up to grasp, but to a child, it was completely inconceivable. I was seven years old, and obviously I knew that if I got a cut, it would bleed. If I fell on the asphalt, I would get a scrape and it would hurt. I knew that people died; I'd seen it. But the only thing I knew on this day that meant anything was that I was hungry.

I was used to being hungry and begging for food. I was used to sniffing glue to deaden the hunger, but when the hunger reached a certain level, it could no longer be deadened. I don't know how long I'd been without food, but I think I hadn't eaten in several days. I remember that it was a sunny day, one of those days when it was really hot in Brazil, one of those days that made it painful to be out in the sun. I was looking for food, just as I'd done on so many other days. I missed Camile, just as I'd missed her every single day since I'd lost her. I can't remember where my mother was, but I think she was looking for work. I found myself in an alley behind some restaurants where there were a bunch of trash cans. There was no one in the alley except me, so I started rummaging through the trash, looking for something to eat, anything at all. It didn't take long before I found a half-eaten piece of flat bread, kind of like a pita bread, with refried beans inside it. I remember being happy, because there was quite a bit of it left. I remember how my mouth watered, and I could imagine what it would feel like to be full after I'd eaten my find.

Startled, I heard a boy's voice say that it was his, that I needed to give it to him—*give him my food!* I told him it was my food, because I'd found it. He could go look in one of the other trash cans. I could tell that he wasn't planning to let me walk away with what I'd found, that there was going to be trouble. I was planning to fight even though he was bigger and older than I was. He walked up to me and tried to take the food out of my hand. I defended myself by kicking and hitting. He took the food anyway, so I bit his hand as hard as I could. He dropped the food, screamed, and punched me hard in the face. We fought, really fought, but it didn't turn out to be a long fight. Even though I used every dirty trick I knew, he was stronger. He pushed me so hard, I fell over one of the trash cans and pulled it over with me as I fell. I scraped my hands, catching myself from the fall, and pebbles and gravel ripped into my palms. I heard a clinking sound next to me. It was a piece of a glass bottle, a big shard. I got up into a sitting position with my hands behind me, one leg still over the trash can. Tons of trash had fallen out, but all I saw was that piece of glass. I picked it up in my right hand. I was mad, sad, and hungry, but most of all I felt like I was being treated so incredibly unfairly. That was my food! I was going to take my food back. I got up and started running at him. He had picked the bread up off the ground and started walking away. I screamed that that was my food and ran at him with all my might. He turned around, and without thinking, still moving, I jabbed that piece of glass at his belly as hard as I could.

He was barefoot like me, and he was wearing jean shorts that came down to his knees and no shirt. I was seven years old, and I'd guess he was eight or nine. He was a little lighter skinned than I was. He had brown eyes, not black like mine. He had short, straight, medium-brown hair and ears that stuck out. He was cute. I remember how he looked at me and how his eyes showed first surprise, then shock, and then pain. The whole time, I kept a firm hold on the piece of glass. At first, I felt nothing. Then I felt my hand getting warm, and at that instant I let go of the shard. The whole thing happened in just a couple of seconds, but my brain remembers it as taking much, much longer. I wish I could say that some bit of reason popped into my head, but all I felt then was fear, fear that I had done something wrong. Then that fear turned into the realization that I truly had done something gravely wrong. I took the bread out of his hand, and he didn't resist. I took it and started to run away. I looked back once as I ran and saw him sitting on the ground, saw how he was screaming and crying. But I didn't hear anything. I ran and ran, putting distance between us.

After I'd run a fair way, I sat down and started eating. The food was completely wasted, though, because as soon as I swallowed the last bite, I started vomiting. I looked at my bloody hand and just vomited and vomited . . . The realization of what I'd done hit me, and I remember thinking, *Forgive me, Camile. Forgive me, God.*

Later, when I heard the other children in the neighborhood talking about the boy who'd been found dead in the alley, I realized what I had done. I didn't say anything to anyone, not even to my mother. If Camile had been alive, maybe I would have talked to her. I heard the children speculating about what had happened to him, and there I was, walking among them, knowing the answer. I decided then that I would never talk about it, never mention it to anyone, because who could love a murderer?

I have never understood violence. What I actually mean is that I've never understood bad people. Violence, on the other hand, is something I can understand. To me, it goes without saying that using violence in self-defense is justified. Using violence to protect someone who's in danger also makes sense to me. I think violence should always be the last resort, but if my or someone else's life is in danger and violence is the last option, that's exactly what I'm going to resort to. Based on my experience, it's hard to reach any other conclusion. I'll never forget a discussion we had in high school in Sweden. The teacher asked us students to discuss and reflect on the death penalty. We had watched a documentary about a man on death row in the US who was waiting for his injection. Discussing the death penalty was not something I wanted to do. Some of my classmates were for it, others against it, and a few thought you couldn't really say for sure. The question was whether it was OK to take another human being's life under certain circumstances.

I had seen enough as a child to be able to say that there are people who should never be allowed to exist among other people. There are people capable of downright evil. You can discuss whether they deserve the death penalty, but what I know most of all is that existence is not black and white. I remember watching my classmates and thinking: *If they only knew what the life of a child on the streets was like—they, who are so sure of what they would do—if only they knew. If they knew what it was like to live with blood on your hands, would they really answer so quickly? How could they know that taking a life can break you down, and that some things once done can never be undone?*

It's hard to say, *I forgive you*, to yourself. It's hard for me to say, "I took someone's life" out loud to myself. The only person who can forgive me is the boy, and he isn't around anymore. Just like me, he wanted to live. How do I carry on? How can I forgive myself? I actually don't know! I try to be a better person, but I'm only human. The greatest comfort I can find is that in my heart, I know that it was never my intention to harm him. I remind myself that I was a child, and the conditions I was living under played a big role in how I acted. At the place I am now in my life, I can look at myself in the mirror, let myself see what's inside me, and still like what I see. I have made my way through all the darkness, and I can like what I see in me, because there's so much good in there, too. If that boy could somehow see me and know how I feel, I believe and hope that he would be able to forgive me.

It's taken me more than twenty years to start talking about what happened, to even be able to mention this to anyone else. The first time I ever talked about it was so liberating, but at the same time, I was incredibly disappointed. I'd read in books and heard people say that the truth will set you free, but it doesn't feel like that to me. On the other hand, I've accepted that it happened. I have forgiven myself in a purely rational sense, although not in an emotional one. That boy has followed me through my life, and I have not allowed myself to forget, for his sake, but also for my own, in order to remind myself of what a human being is capable of under certain circumstances. I don't know if he has a family, someone who misses him, someone who can say something about him, about his life. I feel like I have an obligation to remember him, to bear witness. Had our circumstances been different, his and mine, our biggest problem at that age might have been our parents' getting a divorce or our not getting the Christmas present we wanted. But our reality differed from that of most other children. We were just happy to get one more day.

The only reason I've been able to forgive myself at all is that I know I never meant for that boy to die; I just wanted my food back.

Birthday in Brazil
2015

Rivia and I wake up in our hotel room in São Paulo, and it's my birthday. I'm turning thirty-two. I know that as they get older, many people feel that birthdays aren't such a big deal. And, sure, maybe they're not, but I love having a birthday. I wake up early and contemplate throwing on my workout clothes and sneakers and going for a run in the city. But with my poor sense of direction, I would probably get lost. Instead, Rivia and I decide to take an early-morning walk. As we step out of the hotel, I realize how cold it is. I'm surprised that it's not warmer and hope the sun will start giving off some heat soon. Not only did I pack way too much stuff; I packed the wrong stuff. I didn't bring any warm clothes. It amazes me how differently I behaved before this trip compared to the other foreign travel I've done. I've traveled a fair amount internationally and should have known better, but I was distracted before this trip. I have the world's biggest suitcase—at least it feels that way when I try to lift it. It's full of clothes, but I have nothing to wear. Rivia made the same mistake, minus the gigantic suitcase, which means that I can't borrow clothing from her, either.

We find a little café where we sit down and order baguette sandwiches. We chat, laugh, and also shed a few tears together. This is the first time since I was eight years old that I'm celebrating my birthday on my "home turf." And later today, we're going to visit the orphanage where my brother and I lived for a year before we were adopted.

We found the orphanage online before we came to Brazil. In the days leading up to the trip, I would go to Rivia's house and we would look for clues. I had gone through all the adoption papers, called the Swedish court, the Swedish National Board of Health and Welfare, the Swedish Intercountry Adoptions Authority, the Family Association for Intercountry Adoption, the Brazilian embassy, and the Brazilian consulate.

When I'd almost given up hope, back home at my dad's house in Ramsele, I found an envelope with a logo on it among some old photo albums and stacks of old papers. My Swedish mother Lili-ann was so good about saving everything, like the receipt from Brazil for sandals and baby formula. But she hadn't managed to save the address of the orphanage. This time, though, I felt I might have found it. Rivia looked at the logo on the envelope and told me that it said something about "home for children" on it. She immediately typed the name and address from the envelope into her computer's search program. Suddenly, we found ourselves on the homepage for an orphanage. It was mostly text, and Rivia asked me if we'd found the right one. "I don't know," I replied. However fervently I hoped it would be my orphanage, I wasn't going to allow myself any false hope. I wanted to know for sure. We debated how we could find out if it was my orphanage before we tried contacting them. Rivia's boyfriend, Jens, who was sitting across the kitchen table from us, suggested Google Maps. Rivia typed the address into Google Maps, and a picture of the orphanage filled the screen. I dug back into my memories. I've always been proud at how much I've managed to remember from Brazil, even though I've also been so afraid of my memories. And there I sat, staring at a picture of what could be my old orphanage, and I wasn't sure. I recognized the building, but the colors were different. The little gate into the orphanage wasn't black, as I recalled, but yellow. It seemed smaller in the picture than I remembered it. I asked Rivia if she could navigate us around the building. After a few attempts, we succeeded in making our way around the whole building. All of a sudden, I recognized the hill, the door, and the wall—and I heard myself saying that I was positive this was the orphanage Patrick and I had lived in. I looked at Rivia, tears of relief streaming down my cheeks. This was my orphanage, and I had found a piece of my history on Google Maps.

Now, when Rivia asks me how I feel about going to the orphanage later today, I reply that I'm extremely happy about it. I'm aware of all the emotions churning inside me, but I can't really identify them all. But something tells me that this will be one of my best birthdays ever, that I'll receive the most amazing gift anyone could give me.

The Orphanage
São Paulo, 1990

My mother, my brother, and I had found a small alley where we decided to spread out some cardboard to sleep on. Mamãe and I sat leaning against the gray concrete wall, and she was holding my brother. He was so cute, lying there asleep. He looked really cozy. I wondered if I had been cozy like that, sleeping in her arms when I was little. I must have been, because Mamãe was so nice. Patrique had chubby baby cheeks and short black curls. His arms and legs were plump, and his head was huge compared to the rest of his small body. I wondered if he knew how the world worked, that we didn't have any money or a home. I wondered if he knew who I was and who Mamãe was. There was so much we had to teach him, so much we had to protect him from. The list was long. Mamãe would protect him just as she had protected me, and I would help her.

We sat there quietly. It was a hot night, and the sky was dark. I couldn't see any stars, but I knew they were there. It was so weird that things could exist without being seen. How was it that I could see them one night, but the next night they were gone? Why couldn't I see them during the day? Mamãe said that when daylight came, the sun shone so brightly that the stars couldn't be seen because they were so pale. That sounded logical, but I still couldn't really understand how things could be there but you couldn't see them. She explained to me that love was there, but we couldn't see it; we could only feel it. I sat there in silence for a long time. One of my legs fell asleep. It was unusual for me to be so quiet. She used to say that every day I had a thousand questions and that every day she had to give me a thousand answers.

I looked at my mother, who was just sitting there, staring straight ahead into nothingness. I tried to see what she was looking at, but couldn't figure it out. My eyes returned to my mother, and I realized she was sad. I wanted to make her happy, so I tried to think of something I could do to cheer her up. I always grew worried when she looked sad, so I said the only thing I could think of.

"Mamãe?"

"Yes?"

"Tomorrow, I'm going to get so super-much money that we can buy something really good." I knew that most likely I wouldn't get the money, but I also knew that I would really try. Many times, I wanted to walk into a shop and just take things and run as hard as I could. She had said I could never do that, that I had to promise her that. And I had promised. A promise I have broken and have had to pay a high price for many times.

With a sad smile, Mamãe responded that it was already morning. I didn't understand how it could be the next day, though, because it was still dark. She explained that time was like a circle, that every twenty-four-hour period included both day and night, both light and dark. Then I wondered which came first. How did you know where it started and stopped? She smiled. She looked a little happier, which made me happy.

"You know that clocks are round?"

"Yeah."

"Can I borrow your chalk?"

I had won a piece of chalk in a fight with a boy. I really liked the chalk and often drew on the asphalt with it. I couldn't spell, not even my own name. I was a little sad about that. Camile had said that only rich people could write, that we rats didn't need to since we were never going to be rich. The piece of chalk was almost used up, but I took it out and handed it to my mother. She started by drawing a circle on the ground, and then she wrote in the numbers. At the very top in the middle she wrote twelve and then all the numbers going around until she got back to twelve.

"This is what a clock looks like," she said. I had stolen some watches, so I knew what they looked like, but I'd never considered how they worked.

Then she drew in a zero above the number twelve.

"Mamãe, why are there two numbers at the twelve?"

"Shush! You be quiet now while I explain. Otherwise I'm not going to tell you anything." She gave me a playful smile, which told me she wasn't mad at me, just pretending. I smiled back. "So, my cute, curious, and downright tiresome little monkey, now I'm going to tell you how time works." She sometimes called me a cute monkey because I loved to climb. "We say that a new day begins with the night." I was about to ask a question, but she silenced me with a look. "You see that I wrote a zero at the top."

"Hmm."

"The zero is the start of a new day. Then it's one o'clock, then two, three, four, five, six, seven, and now it's just starting to get light, which means day is beginning. Then the clock keeps going for the daytime. Nine, ten, eleven, twelve. When the clock strikes twelve, that's the middle of the day. Then you start counting from the twelve again. When we get to the one again, then it's one o'clock in the daytime, in the afternoon. Then it's two, three, four, five, six, seven, and then it starts to get dark again. Then the clock turns eight, nine, ten, and eleven. And then you're back to zero. When the clock is back to zero, a new day starts. And then you keep going like that. The clock just starts again. Does that make sense?"

I pondered this for a bit and studied the clock she had drawn for me.

"Mamãe, is one day two trips around the clock?"

"Yes, it is."

"And every number is an hour?"

"Yes, it is."

I started counting from zero to twelve and then counted one more time around. "So, a day is twenty-three hours?"

"No, a day is twenty-four hours. You forgot to count the zero as an hour."

"But, Mamãe, zero isn't anything. You told me that."

"When you're counting on a clock, the zero is also an hour."

"But how can it be when zero is nothing? If I have zero money, then I have no money."

She smiled. She showed me the circle again and had me point to each of the numbers with my finger and count out loud. In the end, I saw that to get to the one again, you had to go past zero. I started counting again. And this time when I got to the zero, I had counted to twenty-four.

"So, what happens to the day once you've counted to twenty-four?" my mother asked me.

I felt a little unsure. Two trips around the clock was one day. So, two new rotations around the clock must be a new day.

"It'll be a new day?" I replied very uncertainly.

"That's right. You're a smart little monkey," she said, smiling. "Now you know how a new day comes into being."

We sat in silence, again, and I thought about how clocks work and felt proud of this new knowledge I now had, very proud. I glanced at my mother. She looked sad again.

"Christiana, there's something I have to tell you, something we need to talk about."

"What?"

"Do you remember how I applied for that job last week? Well, I got the job."

"Oh, you did!" I was thrilled. I knew how hard my mother had been trying to find a job and how sad she was each time one didn't pan out. She'd had to quit her last job because of me, or because of what happened. She had a new job, and I would help her as much as I could.

"I'm going to start working as a maid for a rich family, but I can't take you and Patrique to work with me."

"But, Mamãe, I can help out!"

"I know you can, but the family I'm going to work for won't let me bring my children."

I was sad. I didn't like it when she went away and I had to stay on the streets by myself. I missed Camile. Living alone on the streets left you weak. Who was going to take care of Patrique?

"Mamãe, I can take care of Patrique."

"No, Christiana, I can't leave you alone with Patrique on the streets. It's dangerous. I talked to a children's home that might be willing to take care of him. I'm going there tomorrow, and I'm hoping they'll take him. I'll ask if they can take you, too."

"Are you going to leave us?"

"No, I promise I'll come see you as soon as I can."

I didn't say anything else. She could tell I was sad, and she put her arm around me.

"Christiana, haven't I always come back for you?"

"Yeah . . ."

"Then we'll see each other again. We will always see each other again."

That was all we said that night. I fell asleep with an odd feeling in the pit of my stomach, a kind of feeling I didn't like. It was a feeling of change and not knowing what would happen.

The next day, Mamãe went off and took Patrique with her. For a long time, I sat on our cardboard down that little alley where we'd spent the night. I looked at the clock she had drawn on the asphalt for me. I was mad at her for thinking about leaving us. I was sure she was. I sat there and refused to do anything. I was hungry, but I was too mad to care. After a few hours, my mother returned, without Patrique. She sat down next to me.

"Have you eaten anything?" she asked.

"No!"

"Here you go." She handed me a banana.

"Where's Patrique?"

"He's at the children's home I told you about last night."

"So, you just left him, and now you're going to leave me?" I yelled.

"Christiana, you know I don't want to leave you guys. I love you. But you know how dangerous it is on the streets. Do you want something bad to happen to him?"

"No, I don't want that," I said.

"Where he is now, there are people to take care of him, to give him food and a safe place to sleep every night."

"But I won't get to see him!"

"I talked to the matron, and she said they might be able to take you, too."

"I don't want to go."

"Do you remember what happened to Camile? I don't want that to happen to you. Do you want that?"

"No!"

"Then the children's home is the best I can do for you. Our lives aren't going to get better unless we make some changes, Christiana. When you're older, you'll understand. My life is no life for you, not if there's a chance of something better. We'll see each other all the time, and you'll get to live there. I promise you."

I sat in silence. On some level, I think I understood that she was right. I remembered what had happened to Camile and so many others, but I didn't want to leave my mother. When you love someone, you don't leave them. That's what I thought at the time.

A short while later, the orphanage accepted me. The first thing I did was go see my little brother. He seemed to be doing well. He had his own bed with a railing around it and slept in a room with a bunch of other babies. I stood by his bed and talked to him.

"Mamãe's going to come see us. She said so. She told me to tell you that she'd be back soon. She's going to earn some money so we can be better off, and she promised she wouldn't leave us." As I told him this, I felt the fear creeping in. I was not at all sure of the truthfulness of what I'd just said. I was not at all sure that Mamãe would come back to us. I remembered the look on her face when she left me. She looked sad, and she was crying.

"Christiana, I'll come back. Take care of Patrique and look after yourself. Don't cause trouble. Do you promise me?" This was the last thing she said. I received a long, tight hug from her at the gate. Then the matron escorted me back into the children's home. The gate shut behind me. I looked back and saw her holding the gate with one hand and crying. Tears welled up in my eyes and ran down my cheeks. The matron showed me into her office. She asked me to sit down on a brown chair facing her desk. She eyed me thoughtfully. I wiped away my tears and sat up straight.

"What's your name?"

"Christiana Mara Coelho."

"Do you know why you're here?"

"Because my mother doesn't have any money and because I'm not safe out on the street."

"How old are you?"

"Seven years old."

"How long have you been living on the streets?"

"A long time."

"Do you know what an orphanage is?"

"A home for children who don't have a mother or a father."

She studied me for a bit. It seemed like she was contemplating something. It seemed strange that she was asking me questions she already knew the answers to. She gave me another contemplative look.

"Christiana, do you want to be here?"

It felt like a dangerous question because of the way she'd asked it and because of the tone of her voice. I might not have been the smartest little girl, but I wasn't dumb. I'd been living on the streets too long not to understand that a question, an opinion, could mean much more than just the words that were used. I knew I mustn't give the wrong answer now. If I said that I wanted to be there, I might lose my mother. Maybe I would never get to see her again. But if I said that I didn't want to be there, maybe they would throw me back out on the streets. Patrique would be alone. My mother would be disappointed in me, and I would be breaking my promise to take care of Patrique. I had to answer. If I gave an answer that was neither yes nor no, then I wouldn't be answering wrong, I thought.

"I want to be with my brother, but I really want to see my mother again. I would be sad without them both. But you are so kind, ma'am, to grant us protection from life on the streets." I held my breath. Had I said the right thing? I had answered as nicely as I could, and I looked her in the eye while I answered, so she would know that I was telling the truth. She looked into my eyes for a bit. Then came a question I wasn't prepared for at all.

"Why do you think you and your mother have been living on the streets?"

"Because no one cares about us."

"Why do you think no one cares about you?"

"Because people who have money don't give us anything at all. Because we don't get any jobs and because people hate us."

"Hmm," she said, as if urging me to continue.

"They call us rats and hit us. The police don't care, and they hit us, too."

"That was a hard answer. You seem quite smart for your age. You've had to grow up a little too fast, like so many other children."

She took out some pieces of paper and started jotting down notes. I sat quietly while she wrote. I still wondered if my answer had been right.

"Christiana, you're going to live here starting now. This is your new home for the time being. You'll sleep in a room with other girls your age. Here at the orphanage, there are both girls and boys of various ages, from little babies to a few who are as old as fifteen or sixteen. There are a number of rules you'll have to follow. If you break them, you'll be sleeping on the streets again. Christiana, do you know what rules are?"

"Yes, I know."

"Explain it to me."

"Rules are something everybody has to follow. Rules are decided by the person in charge, and everyone else follows them."

"Exactly! I am the person who makes the decisions here. I am the person in charge. Me and everyone who works here. You will do as you are told. Is that understood?"

"Yes!"

"Causing trouble is not acceptable. We have certain things you need to be on time for. You will go to school, and you will get good grades. Is that understood?"

"Yes!"

"Good! If anything happens, anything serious, I want you to tell me about it, understood?"

"Yes!"

"Good! Then you can go acquaint yourself with your new home."

I felt a little out of sorts. I had a hundred questions, but I knew that I could only ask one. There was only one question that was important. I'd get answers to all the others sooner or later. I tried to figure out the best way to ask the question.

"Excuse me, ma'am. I'd like to know . . . I was just wondering if Patrique and I will get to see our mother again?"

She stood up behind her desk and walked around it to where I was. I felt uncomfortable and had to tilt my head back to be able to look her in the eye.

"Every Sunday, some of the parents come and visit their children. They can stay for a few hours. If your mother wants to and is able to, she knows that she can come see you then. However, I would not count on her coming, Christiana." She gave me a strange, thoughtful look. Then she turned around and started to go.

I followed her in silence. I had dared to ask the question, and it had been answered. She didn't think Mamãe would come visit us. But Mamãe had promised to come. I was confident she would come. Although maybe not entirely confident.

I was scared, so I did what I was good at doing. I stretched my back and pushed my feelings aside and followed the matron into a room crowded with children. When we walked in, the room went quiet, and everyone looked at me. I looked down at my bare feet. From somewhere I heard the matron say that my name was Christiana and that I was going to live here now, and that I would be their new friend.

When I first came to the orphanage, everything was good. I had Sundays to look forward to. And I quickly made a friend. Her name was Patricia, and she became my closest friend in the orphanage. She was the most beautiful girl I'd ever seen. I think she was a year younger than I was, but she could just as easily have been a year older. I know that she told me how she'd wound up in the orphanage, but I can't remember now. Patricia was shy, reserved, and calm—everything I wasn't. She was white, had brown eyes, and her hair was the color of gold with big loose curls. It was cut short like mine. All the kids at the orphanage had short hair, boys and girls, since that made it easier to combat lice. She was nice, and for the most part, the other kids left her alone. She never hurt anyone, and I looked up to her so much. But I couldn't let her in all the way. I hadn't forgotten the feeling of having lost my best friend. I never wanted to feel that again. But Patricia got as close to me as a best buddy can get without getting all the way in. She sang, too. We used to sit together and sing Xuxa's songs. "Ilarie" was our favorite. Xuxa was a woman who had a children's TV show, which we got to watch once a week. Patricia used to laugh when I sang. One time she said that what I lacked in voice I made up for in volume. After many songs and a lot of laughter, I realized she meant that I was off-key. It took me many years to accept that I wasn't going to become the next big singing sensation. Patricia was one of the few people in my life I listened to, really listened to. She had also been going to school and living in the orphanage longer than I had, and I could always rely on her for help.

I was lucky to have Patricia. With so many children in one place, there couldn't be anything but trouble. It gradually became clear to me that there were quite a few rules to follow. The days were very similar. Each started with all the kids gathering outside the shower room in a line to go into the showers, a few of them at a time. There were only a few towels, so you really didn't want to end up toward the back of the line. If you did, you had only cold, wet towels to dry yourself with. Usually the strongest kids and the loudest ones ended up toward the front of the line. I was one of the kids who would wind up in the front, but every day I let Patricia, who was always one of the last in line, go ahead of me. One time I ended up last in the shower line, and I swore that would never happen again. It wasn't really because it was gross to dry yourself off with a cold, wet towel or that all the warm water had been used up. It was more about the principle of the thing, a matter of pride. The system of lining up for the shower and all the other lines we had at the orphanage worked very simply: The stronger child stood in front of the child who was a little weaker. If you wanted to advance in the line, you had to fight the person who stood in front of you. If you won the fight, you could pass the person you'd defeated in the line. Patricia was able to cut ahead, because the kids behind us in line weren't required to fight her, but rather the person who had let her cut—me. If you decided to accept the fight and lost, you risked ending up at the very back.

There was a hierarchy in the orphanage, just like on the streets, and you did not want to be near the bottom. I realized it wasn't going to be that easy for me here. Among the children there were some who really disliked me, because I was a bit of a favorite with the staff. My mother had taught me good manners and how to help out and be nice. Those things will take you far in life. But if you wanted to survive among the kids, you were forced to share with the right kids so that you had some-one who would watch your back, and then you would watch theirs in return. On your own you were weak—that was something you learned fast on the streets. I had always been a little calculating and fairly street-smart, which had sometimes served me well and other times not so well. At the orphanage, it mostly served me well. I also quickly made enemies. Gabriela was one of them.

There were certain unwritten rules at the orphanage. Rule number one: Do not tattle to the staff. Rule number two: Don't make friends with the wrong people. Rule number three: Don't suck up to the staff. Rule number four: Don't own something no one else has (items that the children had received from their families or from the staff would be torn to pieces). Rule number five: Make sure you don't do anything that causes the staff to have to punish you.

These were simple rules that got broken all the time, sometimes by me.

Sunday Is My Favorite Day

Mamãe came to visit my brother and me on Sundays. We met in the backyard out behind the orphanage. There were bushes out there and avocado trees. There was also a kind of stage. The yard was quite big, but we children weren't allowed to go out there very often. But on Sundays we did—those of us who had parents, relatives, or close friends. Some of the kids, ones who didn't have anyone to come visit them, chose to remain inside the orphanage then. Others came outside and jealously and longingly watched the kids who had people who missed them. I loved Sundays. They were good days, and I always longed for them.

Sometimes we kids put on little shows for the people who came to see us. I remember one time we were going to put on a play. We had gotten a book called *Marcelo, Marmelo, Martelo*. The book was about a boy, a shoe, and a hammer. We were going to perform it, and I was super nervous. I had never stood up in front of a group of people and spoken before. Even worse, now I was supposed to do it while pretending to be someone else. I don't remember what part I played. I think that's a little odd given how nervous I was and that I still have the book today. But I was happy, and I wanted to make my mother proud. I wanted to see her smile, and I wanted to be better than all the other kids. Mamãe had always said that if I had my mind set on something, I could do it.

When the other children teased me, and tried to make me nervous before the big day, I thought about what my mother had told me. I could do whatever I wanted if I just made up my mind to do it. And I had decided to be the best. So I read the book over and over again. I read it slowly, very slowly, not so the words would have more or greater significance or so that I would achieve some true understanding. I read slowly because I could barely read.

Sunday approached, and I grew increasingly nervous. All I could think about was that I wanted to make Mamãe proud. I only got to see her a few hours a week, and I wanted her to leave the orphanage feeling like she had a good, talented daughter and feeling like she wanted to come back the following Sunday. The day before we were supposed to perform, we rehearsed in the yard, and while I waited for my turn, I sat by one of the bushes and picked the hard berries that grew there. They looked just like beads. I didn't know what they were called, but you could make bracelets out of them. They were green, almost as hard as rocks, and little, like real beads, but with holes right through them, which made it easy to string them together into a bracelet. I sat there making a bracelet for my mother. I remember that I was trying to figure out how many beads I needed. I mean, Mamãe's wrist was bigger than mine, so if I made the bracelet too small, she wouldn't be able to wear it. On the other hand, it couldn't be too big, either. I didn't finish the bracelet that afternoon, but I had gathered enough beads to finish what I had started later that evening.

That night I wasn't tired at all. I was full of expectation and excitement about the next day and nervous at the same time. I slept fitfully that night. When morning came, I woke up, exhausted.

After we'd showered, gotten dressed, and goofed around like we did most mornings, we headed off to the cafeteria for breakfast. We were wearing the nicest clothes we had. Once I was down in the cafeteria, I sat next to Patricia. I was too nervous to eat anything, so I just drank a cup of coffee with milk and sugar. A lot of sugar! My tummy settled down after the coffee, and I felt a little better. I don't know if it was the coffee or having Patricia there that calmed me down, but she held my hand under the table.

It felt like it took forever for noon to arrive. That was when our parents and relatives could come. With each minute, I grew more and more tense. I tried to slow my breathing and think positive thoughts. And then, finally, the clock struck twelve. All of us kids who were going to be in the play were already out in the backyard. Any of the other kids who wanted to were allowed to come outside, too, and today quite a lot of the kids without relatives had come outside. They wanted to watch the play. Some of them were there because they thought it would be fun, others to see if any of us made fools of ourselves onstage. Gabriela was there with her little clique. She looked at me and jeered. As I walked by her, she hissed, "Good luck, you fucking rat! Do your best—you're going to be a disaster."

The kids' families poured in, and I searched for my mother. I was going to run to her the way I did every Sunday and give her a bear hug, and she would hug me back just as tight. But I didn't see her. Everyone had come in, and there wasn't anyone else coming through the gate. Where was my mother? Why hadn't she come? Had I done something wrong? Maybe she was just a little late. That must be it. Mamãe was running a little late. I sat by my bead bush and waited and waited until finally I realized that she wasn't going to show up. For some reason, she didn't want to or couldn't. I sat and watched the other kids, who all looked so happy. The air was filled with laughter and hugs. I sat there, sad, and watched all the love that was there, right in front of me. Now I understood how the other children felt, the ones no one ever came to visit. I wondered why my mother hadn't come.

"Oh, poor little Christiana! Did your whore of a mother abandon you?" Gabriela hissed. I got so mad, it was all I could do not to jump her in front of all the parents. Had I done that, the punishment would have been extreme, so I just glared at her. "You know what?" Gabriela continued. "We know where your mother is. She's out whoring around on the streets and doesn't give a shit about you."

I got up, on the verge of pouncing on her and knocking out all her teeth, but I just said, "You're going to regret saying that." I turned on my heel and started walking away from her and her clique.

"I guess you're looking for an ass-whooping, huh?" she yelled after me, and they all laughed.

I was so mad, so sad, and so disappointed in my mother. I heard the matron talking to all the children and grown-ups gathered in the backyard. She was standing on the stage and explaining that we children had put together a play and that we were going to perform it now. Ugh, I just wanted to run away and hide! But I knew I couldn't do that. That would just give Gabriela and her clique more to tease me about. The last thing I remember about that evening was walking up onto the stage.

I kept my promise to myself. As soon as I saw Gabriela, I jumped her. A lot of kids saw this happen and quickly formed a ring around us. I was glad that so many people were watching, because I wanted as many people as possible to see Gabriela's humiliation. As I pummeled her, I yelled, "I'm going to kill you! I'm going to kill you!" And for the first time in my life, I felt like I really meant it.

"Are you mad because I called your mother a whore? Why are you mad about that? Because that's exactly what she is!" she taunted me.

That did it. There was no stopping me now. I jumped on her again and pushed her down onto the cold, hard floor. Somewhere in the background, I heard children yelling and cheering. I didn't care. We lay there, wrestling on the floor, and I knew that no matter what happened, I was going to win. I managed to get her lying on her back, and I was straddling her stomach. She was kicking and trying to twist me off her, but I was too heavy. I was holding both her hands and managed to get her left arm under my right knee. I held her other arm and swung my free arm into the air. I remember the fear in her eyes. I assume what she saw in me was pure hatred. I punched her in the face. Blood spurted from her nose, but I didn't care. She screamed loudly, and I hit her again, as hard as I could. I managed to get in one more blow before one of the staff members grabbed me from behind and pulled me off Gabriela. I was kicking and thrashing and screaming that I was going to kill her.

"Just you wait! When you least expect it, I'm going to come kill you!" I roared.

What would eventually frighten me, when I got a little older, was the fact that I didn't know whether I would have stopped hitting her if that woman who worked at the orphanage hadn't dragged me off Gabriela. I was so filled with hatred and at the time so blinded by it that I had no thought other than killing her. Every single cell in my body wanted to see her suffer, wanted to see her eradicated from the surface of the earth, wanted people like her to be annihilated. I had encountered so many mean, spiteful people, and I felt forlorn. I'm glad that orphanage lady got there when she did.

She held me, and I calmed down a bit. I looked at Gabriela and felt better. There was blood everywhere, and a sense of satisfaction spread through me. The woman asked who had started the fight. She hadn't decided yet which of us to punish. Gabriela lay there bleeding. She looked awful, but the woman knew that the person who started the fight was the one who needed to be punished. It was always like that. The staff would make an example of whoever started it to scare us kids away from breaking the rules. She asked again and reminded all the kids that if they didn't tell her who'd started the fight, everyone would get a beating.

Total silence.

All the kids standing there were afraid of me now. They knew that whoever blabbed was going to get it from me. But I also knew that if I didn't step forward and say it was me, the kids who got punished would hate me. So I did what was smartest. Not because it felt right, but because I had calculated that this would keep kids from being punished and then they would be grateful. It would show that I wasn't afraid of the employees and was brave enough to take the pain. And I knew that people would think twice before messing with me.

Gabriela was taken away and bandaged up. I knew what awaited me. A lot of kids had gathered around, not just the younger ones but the older ones, too. The woman who'd stopped the fight asked me why I'd started it. I didn't answer. She asked again, and this time her voice sounded ice-cold. I didn't answer. I held my head up high as best I could.

I was trying to show that I wasn't scared and that I was proud. I wasn't planning to answer her question. I knew I was making my situation worse by being defiant and not answering, but I was ready to accept the consequences. I wasn't about to repeat what Gabriela had said about my mother, not out loud in front of all these kids. Even if they didn't dare tease me, they would still whisper about it behind my back. I refused to say things about my mother that weren't true.

The woman asked me to remove my T-shirt and pants. I stood in front of all the kids in just my underpants, and she held one of my hands so I stood with my back to her. In her other hand she held a belt, which she whipped my back and legs with. I tried to run away from her, but her grip on my hand let her pull me in closer. This resulted in my just running around and around and around her while she whipped me with the belt. I tried to jump out of the way, to run away. I tried to duck from the blows, but it was useless.

It hurt. A lot. I couldn't sleep on my back that night. I couldn't even sit down. My whole body was swollen. I had open wounds on my back and legs that burned, and some of them were oozing blood, but I didn't regret a thing. I had this sense that my mother would not have approved of what had happened, that she would not have been pleased with my behavior, but I didn't care. Why should I? She had let me and Patrique down. She hadn't come to see us even though she promised. She'd left me, which she had promised never to do. I cried quietly to myself. The woman had told me to ask for forgiveness, to say I wouldn't do it again, but I refused. It wasn't because I was too proud at that moment. Believe me, the whipping hurt so much that I would have done almost anything that she asked. But she'd asked me to apologize for hitting someone who deserved to be hit. I was supposed to admit that I had done the wrong thing and that my mother was everything Gabriela had said, but I refused to do that. I thought Gabriela deserved the beating she got.

My opinion on this has changed over the years, and I no longer feel anything but sorry for her, and for Christiana. We both lived in a world where such strong, hateful emotions were part of our everyday lives. Children should not grow up like that, and I would give so much now to learn what Gabriela had been through before she ended up in the orphanage. No child can live with so much hatred and so much rage without a reason. I should know. If I'd had a little less rage and frustration in me when I was eight, as an adult I wouldn't have wondered if my eight-year-old self would have ever stopped pummeling that girl, had no one intervened. A girl who, like me and all the other street kids, deserved so much more, so much more love and so much more of life.

Later, in my life in Sweden, I met a Brazilian woman who asked me where in Brazil I was from and where I'd lived. I replied that I'd lived in the slums and was a street child. She looked at me, smiled, and said, "Oh, street children are so happy. They have a genuine enthusiasm."

What do you say to that? She wasn't wrong. There is incredible joy in these children, but there are also unbelievable pain and sorrow.

Why Can't I See Mamãe?

After that big fight with Gabriela, the matron summoned me to her office so I could explain what had happened, why I'd started the fight.

I didn't lie. She listened and when I was done, she just said that she understood that I'd been angry, but that my behavior was unacceptable. She said that she never wanted to hear that I'd behaved that way again. Then she said that I would not get to see my mother anymore, that she was no longer welcome to come and see me and my little brother. The reason Mamãe hadn't come to see us that Sunday was that she was no longer welcome.

I couldn't understand what she was saying . . . What? I mean, Mamãe had come to see us every Sunday, just as all parents were allowed to do. I knew that Mamãe wanted to come see us. Why wouldn't she come see us anymore? Had I done something wrong, something bad? Did the matron know that I'd picked avocados from the trees outside and hidden them in the fridge in the kitchen? Was she punishing me now for taking the avocados? My little brother wasn't going to get to see Mamãe because of me. I was so upset. I tried to hold back my tears, but it was hard. As usual when I tried to keep from crying, a tear ran down my cheek. I was forced to ask if I'd done something wrong.

"No, Christiana. You haven't!"

"But why are you punishing me and my brother? I've tried to be nice, and I've tried to help out. I've been doing my best at school. Why can't I see my mother again?"

"I'm not punishing you. I'm trying to help you!"

"So, my mother does get to come see us again?"

"I didn't say that. You understand, Christiana, your mother is sick. She's very sick."

"My mother didn't tell me she's sick! She's doing well! She has a job, and she buys me things."

The matron was quiet for a moment. She seemed to be thinking. She took a deep breath, sitting there behind her desk, then pulled her hand through her straight, black hair. She usually wore her hair up in a ponytail, but today it was down. She was wearing a white blouse and a light matching skirt. She said my name, but I scarcely heard it. She had said that Mamãe was sick. Why would she say that? Mamãe always told me everything, and she had hardly ever lied to me. I heard my name again and looked up.

"Christiana, your mother has a mental illness. Do you know what that means?"

I had no idea what that meant, but I'd heard of it before. My mother had explained to me that I had two older brothers, twins. One was named Humberto, and I can't remember the other one's name, but I've always called him Gilberto. My mother had said that they'd been born a little "funny," that they had a mental illness.

I'd asked her what that meant, and she had said that they were just a little different. But she loved them, too.

Now here sat the matron, telling me that my mother was "funny." But Mamãe wasn't "funny." I knew my mother, and she wasn't "funny."

"Christiana, we've decided that she isn't good for you, you or your little brother. We've decided that she can't come to see you anymore. We've already explained this to her."

I couldn't take any more. I was furious with the matron. How could she do this to me? I always helped out—in the kitchen, with the babies, with the laundry and the cleaning. All of it so they would like me, and yet she was still punishing me. Life was so fucking unfair. The rage grew in me until I practically exploded and screamed.

"My mother is not 'funny'! You can't decide if I get to see her or not! You're the devil, and I hate you! I hope you burn in hell forever!"

The matron stiffened. She looked surprised—she'd never seen me act like this. Every single time I was punished for having started a fight or misbehaving in some way, every single time they beat me, I had accepted it. I screamed when they beat me because it hurt, but I refused to cry. Many of the children screamed in pain and cried when they were beaten. To me, crying in front of other people was a sign of weakness, and I had learned that showing weakness didn't get you anywhere in this world. People were just even nastier and would abuse and exploit you if you showed them you were vulnerable. I wasn't going to let anyone see me that way. My pride wouldn't allow it. And I was not planning to give the people beating me the satisfaction of knowing that they'd hurt me.

Here I stood now in the matron's office, being punished for no reason. I hadn't done anything wrong, and still I was being punished. Did she think I was just going to accept their taking my mother away from me? I'd already lost so much that I loved. Just then, I detested her more than anything else. I screamed again how much I hated her, and opened the door and ran out of her office. I heard her calling my name and asking me to stay, telling me to come back. But I just ran as fast as I could.

When I got angry like that, I had a tendency to black out. It wasn't until I calmed down that I could think again. In the middle of the rage, I felt nothing but hatred. That part of me frightened both me and other people when I was little, especially when I moved to Sweden. Sture, my Swedish dad, once told me, "Christina, you have unbelievably beautiful eyes. But when you're mad, they turn completely black, like a witch's. It scares me."

Maybe it's not so unusual that I couldn't control that part of myself when I was little. I was carrying around so much that was so tremendously painful. I had no one to talk to who could help me deal with the pain, the grief, and the bitterness, feelings that can be hard enough to deal with as an adult. Instead, I would curl up in some corner where no one would see me, and cry. I let the pain run out of me, and then I sat there, silent and snotty-nosed and teary-eyed, and lost myself in my dreams.

I dreamed myself away into some of Camile's fairy-tale worlds, where we rode horses or won soccer games. Where we could talk to the animals and eat however much candy and food we wanted. I dreamed that Mamãe and I were sitting on a cloud somewhere in the sky, gazing down at Brazil. We would fly around and get up to a ton of mischief, the way we used to out in the woods. I fantasized about living with the angels and the peace and beauty of their country.

I did eventually calm myself down after my outburst at the matron. When I came back to reality, I found myself sitting on a toilet lid with my arms around my legs. I had picked up my legs so no one would see that I was in the stall. I had locked the door and sobbed in silence. I remember that I was exhausted, completely drained of energy, and that life felt hard. I remember that I didn't want to exist. I wanted to be like the stars in the daytime—there, but not visible. I didn't want anyone to see me or talk to me. All I wanted was to be with my mother and my little brother. I wanted to be in the woods where I could play, climb, run around, and swim. I don't know how long I sat there. Every now and then, I heard a child come in and use one of the other toilets. I sat completely still and held my breath. Gradually my brain started working again. I tried to digest what had happened, what had been said. And even though I had meant every word I'd said to the matron, I understood that it hadn't been very smart of me to lose my temper that way. Then I started thinking. There must be a way for me to see my mother again. Maybe I could run away. But the walls were too high to climb over, and the gates were always locked. The only time they let us out was when we went to the school, which wasn't very far from the orphanage. I might be able to run away while we were at school, run as hard as I could before anyone noticed. As I sat there plotting my escape, I happened to think of Patrique. I couldn't just leave him behind. Mamãe wouldn't forgive me. Who would take care of him? I totally loved him, so how could I leave him behind? He was just a baby who couldn't run, couldn't think. How could I run away and bring him with me?

I became frustrated. The plan I had come up with wouldn't work. I couldn't leave the orphanage without Patrique. And I had no idea how I could bring him with me. Even if I managed to sneak out of my room and get him, what would I do then? I could try to steal a couple of keys. I was quite good at picking pockets. I could enlist a few of the other kids, the ones I trusted, to help me. They could distract some of the employees while I swiped their keys. But they would surely discover it before they left for the day. I could talk to Patricia about it, and we could come up with something together. Maybe she could come along and live with me, Mamãe, and Patrique. I felt my brain kicking into overdrive. I would get some food, enough for several days. I would keep doing my best in school. I would act like nothing was going on, and when they least suspected it, Patrique and I would be gone.

I came out of the bathroom, walked back to the matron's office, and knocked on her door. I heard her yell, "Come in." I opened the door, bowed my head slightly, and let my shoulders fall forward. I probably looked like a dog with its tail between its legs. I walked into her office and apologized for yelling at her, and I also apologized for running off. I said it was just that I missed my mother.

The tears came, and I was mad at myself for not being able to hold them back.

The matron came around from behind her desk and gave me a hug. She said she understood that I missed my mother but that everything would be good again, everything would be much better now. My only thought was that if I'd had a knife, I'd have stabbed her in the back.

Then I went up to see Patrique and picked him up out of his crib. I held him tight, and he didn't really seem to like it, so I loosened my grip a little. I held him in my arms and rocked him back and forth. As I rocked him, I whispered, "Patrique, I'm going to find a way for us to get out of here. We're going to see Mamãe again. I'm going to think of a plan, because you have a smart sister."

What I didn't know, what it was impossible for me to know, was that the matron already had plans for me. These plans included my leaving the orphanage, but not to go back to Mamãe, not to return to my world. I never got the chance to try to run away, and maybe that was lucky. As a child, I never understood how much the matron cared about me, how good her intentions toward me and my brother were. When I got older, Lili-ann and Sture told me that the matron had called them numerous times to check on how we were doing during the five weeks we stayed in São Paulo while arrangements were being made for the adoption and our departure for Sweden. It made me happy to hear that. Despite everything, I had many nice memories of my time in the orphanage.

With Thirty Boxes of Chocolates in My Arms
2015

Rivia and I walk out of the hotel and get into the car that's going to take us to the orphanage. If I'd been sitting in this car ten or fifteen years earlier, there'd have been quite a bit of rage left in me. Now I don't feel it; I haven't felt it for a very long time. We sit in the car, knowing that the trip will take about an hour, depending on traffic. With twenty-two million people living in the greater São Paulo area, you can always expect heavy traffic. We've asked the driver to stop at a candy store close to the orphanage. I am not planning to show up empty-handed. Back home in Sweden, I wavered for a long time about what to give the kids at the orphanage. In the end, I decided to give them each a box of chocolates. I settled on that after thinking about what had made me happy in the orphanage. I will never forget the box of Bon O Bon brand chocolates Mamãe brought me when she came to visit. I was so happy! I know that a box of chocolates won't change the children's lives or their futures, but maybe they will feel the same joy in the moment that I did as a child.

I look out the car window at the gigantic highway we're on. A bus squeezes by, going much too fast. I definitely prefer the traffic in Sweden, even if I personally drive like I live in São Paulo. We've left the part of the city with the skyscrapers and the big galleries, and are now greeted by smaller buildings, little shops, and big wooden telephone poles with a crazy number of electrical wires, a design that looks extremely dangerous. We exit the big highway and drive on smaller streets. People are strolling along the streets in their flip-flops, and we drive past a coconut stand where someone is selling coconut water. Someone else is selling whole ears of corn on the cob, and everything feels familiar to me. It's hard to describe, but it's like I know this world, and yet at the same time it feels so foreign.

The driver stops the car outside a shop. We climb out and go into the shop to look for my Bon O Bon candies. I walk past several shelves, and then I see them, the yellow boxes of chocolates. They look almost exactly like I remember them. I show Rivia that I've found them, pick up one of the boxes, and look at it. It feels smaller as I hold it now than it did twenty-four years ago. I smile and feel my eyes well up; it's ridiculous to cry because I'm holding a box of chocolates, but that's what I do. Eagerly, I start loading my arms full of boxes. We realize that I'm not going to be able to carry all the boxes, so Rivia approaches one of the employees to ask if we can get a big cardboard box to put them in. There are about twenty children living at the orphanage, so I put about thirty boxes in the cardboard box, and we load that into the car. We don't have far to go now, and during that brief trip, I can't help but wonder why there are only twenty children at the orphanage. When I lived there, there must have been two to three hundred. Not that I'd counted them all, but there were definitely more than twenty of us.

I know that many of my memories are reliable, but I also know that children experience things differently. For example, I remember when my mother and I wandered into Diamantina during Carnival. I remember seeing the devil come dancing down the street. My mother had told me many stories about God and Jesus and the devil. And there he was, dancing in the street, and I was terrified that he was going to get me. I remember how I hid behind Mamãe. For a long time, I believed I had actually seen the devil. Something that felt so real to me when I was four became unreal to me as an adult, and I can laugh at it now. But that doesn't change how I experienced it at the time. So, as I climb back into the car with all my boxes of chocolates, I ask myself, *Am I remembering wrong? How many of us kids were there?* I've been so afraid of my memories but have also relied on them, and it's extremely important to me now that I'm back that they're correct.

We get out of the car, and I stand outside the orphanage and wait. I look at the little yellow gate in front of me. In my day, the gate was black. The yellow paint has come off in a few places, and where it has, I see the black paint shining through. I realize that I'm still compulsively clutching the gate.

Eight Years Old and Alone in the World
1991

I really didn't know what had happened. What had changed? I don't know why they thought my mother wasn't a good mother. I only know that someone decided that I didn't get to be her daughter any longer, that they took strong and decisive action to keep us from seeing each other and to keep my mother from coming near me.

After the matron explained to my mother and me that we wouldn't get to see each other anymore, life at the orphanage became really tough. I remember when it started. One day, a sunny Sunday, when the kids were visiting with their relatives in the backyard, the other kids, the ones who didn't have anyone to come visit them, started running around. Some were whispering and some were yelling, and they were all in high spirits. Something out of the ordinary was obviously going on, and all the fuss got Patricia and me curious. We followed the stream of other kids. It seemed as if something was happening by the front door of the orphanage. A lot of kids were clustered around the gate, and we were at the very back of the crowd, so we couldn't see anything. The employees were yelling for everyone to back up and return inside.

Patricia asked one of the girls standing next to us what all the commotion was about. The girl said that apparently a parent was standing at the gate and yelling for one of the kids. Patricia stiffened and looked at me. We were thinking the same thing, and her hand had already found mine and was holding it tight. I can't explain how I knew. Maybe it was the mother-daughter bond that gave off a special energy that only the two of us could feel. Maybe it was all the love my mother had given me, which gave me the knowledge deep down inside that she loved me despite everything that had happened. But I just knew that it was my mother who was standing outside the gate. I started pushing my way through the crowd and yelling for the kids to move. As I neared the gate, I could hear her voice. I'd never heard my mother yell like that. It was a desperate yell, full of fear, rage, and helplessness. I could hear that she was yelling for me:

"Christiana, where are you? I want to see my daughter! I have a right to see my daughter! *Christiana!*"

"She's not here!" an angry-sounding woman's voice responded.

"I know she's here! You can't take her away from me!" my mother replied. She continued to yell hysterically for me.

It hurt so much, and yet relief washed over me. My mother had come. She hadn't abandoned me at all. She loved me. She was here now. I was running, pushing my way through, up to the gate, and then I saw her. She had completely lost it. She was crying and screaming; I had never seen her so upset. I started yelling for my mother, but a hand grabbed me. Just then, I heard my mother scream my name again. The hand stopped me, and one of the women who worked there held on to me firmly. I was upset and frustrated and extremely angry. I kicked the woman as hard as I could in the shin and hit her face with my free hand. She lost her grip on my arm, and I ran up to the gate. I reached my hands out to my mother's and felt her hands in mine.

"Mamãe!"

"Christiana!"

"Mamãe!" I was wailing and sobbing, and my mother was crying.

I felt a woman grab me and hold me tight. My mother's hold on my right hand grew firmer, and I grasped the gate with my left hand. The woman started pulling me away from the gate. I held on to Mamãe and the gate with all my might, and Mamãe held on to my hand. She shouted at the woman to let me go, and I cried out to Mamãe over and over again. I yelled at the woman to let go of me. I kicked at the air and tried to wriggle out of her hold. Another woman came over and grabbed my left hand and ordered me to let go of the gate. I yelled, "No!" over and over, and Mamãe kept hollering for them to let me go, that they should leave me be.

One of the women started prying up my fingers one by one to get me to let go of the gate. I yelled and yelled. It was hurting my fingers, but I kept trying to hold on. She was forced to use both hands to undo my grasp, and she yelled at me to stop my foolishness. I screamed that I hated her. She yelled to some of the children that they should come help. I managed to get my left hand free from the other woman's grasp, and I was holding Mamãe's hands tightly again with both of my hands. The children were tugging on me now, too, and in the end, the two women managed to separate my hands from Mamãe's. They picked me up and Mamãe yelled to me and I yelled back. I heard Mamãe yell that she loved me, and I yelled back. I hit and kicked at anyone and anything I could get at. While they carried me through the sea of children, I heard Mamãe's yelling get quieter and quieter until I couldn't hear her voice anymore. The last thing I heard was the matron telling all the children to move away from the gate. At that moment, I hated her. I hated all the employees and all the children. I was more than mad; I was filled with hate. I wanted to hurt everyone, because everyone hurt me, and I didn't understand why. I screamed, and then I don't remember anything more.

When I woke up in my bed, I was huddled in a fetal position. Patricia was sitting next to me, and I could see that she'd been crying. She asked me how I was. I didn't respond, just shook my head. My throat hurt, my head hurt, my eyes hurt, my body hurt. My fingers ached, and I was completely exhausted. But what hurt most of all was my heart. I started thinking about what had happened, about how Mamãe had stood there, yelling and crying and trying to hold on to me. I started sobbing again, and Patricia stroked my hand. I didn't go down to dinner, and she sat with me the whole time. I cried and slept, woke up and cried, slept and woke. It was like that for the rest of the evening. Patricia sat with me the whole time. When it was time for the other children who slept in the same room as I did to go to bed, they came into the room in silence. I heard them whispering, and I pretended I was asleep. The lights were turned off, and then it was dark. The whispering gradually died away, and the children slept. I lay awake and cried, but I tried to cry silently. Patricia heard me anyway and asked if she could get into bed with me. I said yes, and she lay next to me and held me.

So many nights I've had nightmares about what happened that day. This memory and these feelings are hard to express in words. They ripped me away from my own mother and didn't explain anything to me. I was almost eight years old and completely brokenhearted. My feeling of loneliness grew stronger. Most of all I felt, and still feel, sorry for my mother. I don't have any children myself, but the thought of someone physically tearing my child away from me makes my heart ache. There are no words strong enough to describe how horrifically cruel what they did to me and my mother was on that day and the days that followed.

When I woke up the next day, Patricia was lying beside me with her arm around me. I was tired, broken, and empty. All of the children got up, but very few looked my way. Those who did had pity in their eyes. I hated that and pretended I didn't notice. I wasn't going to show them how upset I was. Gabriela and her clique sneered at me; I could handle that. I felt hatred for them, and that made the whole thing easier. I wanted no part of the other children's feeling sorry for me. It was enough that I felt sorry for myself. I didn't want to be reminded of that by everyone else around me. Patricia and I walked to the bathroom and got into the shower line. Everyone pretty much knew their places, and there wasn't any fuss today. It went quickly: into the shower, out of the shower, dry off quickly on the damp towel, get dressed. We went downstairs and ate breakfast. I can't remember a single breakfast from the orphanage. I have no idea what we ate. All I remember is the coffee with a lot of milk and sugar.

After we'd eaten, it was time to go to school. We walked to the gate where the matron stood waiting with one of the employees. Something was wrong. The matron wasn't usually at the gate when we left for school. Once all the children had gathered, she called me over. I felt a little confused. Why did she want to see me? What had I done wrong now? I walked up to her, and she gestured with her hand that I should stand next to her. Then she started talking to the children. She explained to the children that they should form several rings around me and that we should walk to school like that. I would be in the middle, and around me would be a ring of about five or six children, all of them holding hands. And around the first ring, the children would form another ring, then another, and finally one last ring outside that one. All the children in the rings would hold hands. She was building a jail out of children around me. The matron showed the children where to stand: the youngest would be in the innermost circle and the eldest and strongest children would be in the outermost ring. She continued her instructions, and the words that followed came as a shock to me. She explained to the children that under no circumstances could they let go of one another's hands or let my mother get to me.

The matron said that if they let my mother close to me, they would be punished. I stood there completely flabbergasted in the middle of the first ring, still not properly grasping what was happening. The gates were opened, and we started walking to school, with me in the middle and the children hand in hand in circles around me. We were about halfway to school when I heard my mother call my name. I turned around and saw her come running toward me. The children started walking faster, and I noticed that some of them looked worried. My mother called to me several times, and when she reached us, she yelled very clearly that they should let her through. The children were walking fast now, and I was being pushed along. Mamãe was crying and she started tugging on the children's hands and arms. The children shoved her away; I yelled for them to stop, yelled for them to let her through. I tried to push my way through to Mamãe, but there were too many children blocking me. I saw how some of the children were kicking her and pushing her away.

The image of my crying mother desperately trying to reach me has been another nightmare that has followed me my whole life. The distress I saw in her eyes and felt in my heart is among the most painful things I've ever seen or felt.

We reached the school, and the staff there met us and helped the other children drag me into the school. The gate was closed, and I could hear Mamãe crying and howling that they couldn't do this, that they couldn't take her child away from her. That day at school I did nothing. At recess, the other children played in the school yard. It was paved, and there was a climbing structure where I had dedicated many recesses to perfecting my climbing technique and balance. There were three swings, which the children fought over. But on this day, I spent recess crying in a corner in the hallway.

I didn't understand why they were doing this to me and Mamãe. I didn't understand how everyone could be so cruel. For all the world, I couldn't understand how they, all of them—the matron, the orphanage and school staff, the children—could be so cruel to my mother. All the other children who had parents or a relative got to visit with them. Why was it any different for me and my mother? When school ended, the children encircled me again, and we walked back to the orphanage. A part of me was happy that this time my mother didn't show up. Seeing her so sad and not getting to be with her was terribly painful. When we reached the orphanage, the circles around me dissolved, and one of the women asked the children how everything had gone. I didn't stick around to listen, but as I was walking, I saw some of the children who'd been in the outermost circle glaring at me.

When evening came, four of these children sought me out. There was a fight. I wish I could say that I won, but the truth is, I took a licking. When the fight ended, the children said they expected my "damn mother" not to cause any problems the next day.

All I could think was, *The next day? This is going to happen all over again tomorrow? How long is this going to go on?*

That night, as I lay in bed, I tried to figure out how I could successfully escape from the orphanage.

I fell asleep and woke up tired. I had a terrible headache, and my knuckles were sore from the previous evening's fight. It was Tuesday, and the routines this morning looked the same as the routines the day before and all the other days: we showered, got dressed, and ate breakfast. When it was time to go to school, to my great horror, the same procedure from the day before was repeated. The children formed rings around me, and we left the orphanage. Mamãe showed up and tried to reach me, and I tried to get to her. That night I got beaten up again. The same thing happened for the entire week. Every day, sobbing and yelling, Mamãe tried to get to me, and every day, I tried to get to her. I spent recesses crying in the same hallway corner. I didn't do any homework, and I refused to eat any food. I didn't talk to anyone except my friends, who also got beaten up for siding with me or fighting on my behalf.

By Friday, I was a physical and mental wreck. The whole week, whenever she walked by me, Gabriela whispered into my ear that my mother was crazy and that I was the child of a whore. I didn't say anything. I ate for the first time, but I still didn't talk to anyone except Patricia. She had held me and cried with me many times. When night fell and all the other children were asleep, I lay awake.

I got up and snuck over to Gabriela's bed. I clenched my right fist tight, pulled my arm back, and then punched her as hard as I could in the face. I hit her cheek, and she woke up shrieking. I hit her again and again. All the children woke up, and it ended in a huge brawl with everyone fighting. Gabriela took a real licking from me, and with every punch I landed on her, a small portion of my anger seemed to melt away. Hitting felt good. An orphanage employee, awakened by the noise of the brawl, ran into our room. Most of the fighting stopped then, but Gabriela and I kept hitting each other.

When the woman managed to separate us, she asked who had started it. I screamed that it was Gabriela, and she screamed that it was me. The woman looked at the other children, hoping that one of them would provide the answer, but she was met with silence. Many of the kids probably had no idea who had started it, and the few who did knew better than to blab. I came out with a lie. I said that Gabriela was mad at me because my mother had tried to take me out of the orphanage, that my mother had hit her, and that that was why she wanted to get back at me. Gabriela said I was lying. The woman chose to believe me. I don't know whether it was because I lied well or because she wanted to put an end to all the fuss. Maybe she chose my version because she knew what a tough week it had been for me and that I didn't need a whipping right then. When Gabriela was allowed to get back into bed, she looked over at me, and I flashed her one of my biggest smiles. The woman turned off the light after a couple of carefully chosen words about how if she so much as heard a peep from this room, every child in it would get a taste of her belt. It was dead quiet in the room. We heard the door close. I fell asleep that night with a cozy feeling, and I remember that when I woke up on Saturday morning, I was well rested. After that, Gabriela didn't dare go after me again.

I started to realize I was going to have to give in. I was going to be forced to play a role. I stopped contradicting the other children, and sometimes I agreed with them to avoid trouble. The orphanage was too dangerous for me, both physically and mentally, if I didn't conform. I couldn't risk losing my spot in the pecking order. I cried at night and prayed to God for forgiveness, and during the day I played along. I just couldn't fight it anymore. I couldn't take being beaten up all the time, and I couldn't take watching my friends being beaten up and leaving me one by one. I started playing a convincing part, a part that was based on agreeing with all the kids that my mother was crazy. I started feeling embarrassed in front of the other kids that my mother was standing outside the gate yelling. Only Patricia knew how I really felt and how sad I was. There's a limit to how many beatings and how much pain and sorrow one person can handle. Maybe it was weak of me to give in, but I realized that I couldn't stand up for my mother anymore.

What was even worse was that just not defending her anymore wasn't enough. I went farther and pretended I agreed with them that there was something wrong with her. I knew better, but I couldn't take any more. I realized this was a battle I was never going to win, so I decided to always hold on to the truth in my heart while false words about how bad my mother was came out of my mouth. From the beginning, every unkind word I said pained me. I said them only when I was backed into a corner. After a while, I learned to build a strong wall around my heart, one that prevented those wicked words from penetrating. I started satisfying the orphanage staff's need to know how much I didn't want to be with my bad mother and how they were doing the right thing. On some level, I began to understand that people, especially grown-ups, weren't interested in the truth but rather in a truth that suited them. They only wanted to know about things that made stuff easier for them. It didn't matter that I was walling off parts of myself, that I was turning into someone else, a worse person. It wasn't important to them whether I was happy, or whether I cried myself to sleep each night. No one saw it. For the first time in my life, I started to question why I existed, why I should even care about existing. After all, no one seemed to be interested in what I thought and felt, so why should I?

Apart from my friends at the orphanage, the people who cared about me were either dead or had been cast out of my life. I thought again and again about why this was happening to me. What had I done to deserve all this? I prayed to God for forgiveness every night. I prayed to God to protect my mother and my little brother. After a while, I stopped praying to God for forgiveness and instead just prayed for my mother and my little brother to be all right, for them to be happy. I started to realize that happiness wasn't something for me. It was a strange sensation to have at the age of eight, the feeling that I wasn't worth anything. I couldn't show who I was, and wasn't supposed to feel what I felt. And now I didn't have my mother's love.

Up to this point, I had always been able to be myself. It didn't matter if I was with my mother, with friends, or with people I didn't know. I had always been able to be myself. This new realization that my feelings, thoughts, and desires should be suppressed was very uncomfortable. As if it were yesterday, I remember the sensation of a warm, humid, sticky fog closing in around my body, as if I were being wrapped in plastic wrap. Even though the fog was uncomfortable, it had its advantages. One thing that's quite certain is that while I was at the orphanage, although I had already begun to build a façade, I tenderly and adamantly held on to the core of myself inside the fog. Christiana was lost in the fog, but she wasn't dead; one day the fog would burn off, and she would find her way home again.

Two strong survival strategies, which for a long time came to be the most important in my life, were established at the orphanage. They both began on the streets, but it was at the orphanage that they evolved.

Strategy number one was my façade—my ability to adapt and lie. The second was the ability not to lose the joy and beauty that was in me—not to become a ghost. Of course, these strategies have had their pros and cons. They were what so obviously cleft my soul and my self in two. Christiana was hidden in the fog, and a new person emerged, the girl who eventually came to be called Christina.

Later, my Swedish parents and I learned from a Brazilian teacher that many children adopted after a certain age couldn't handle the adjustment. They became, in his words, either crazy or unresponsive. I think the only way for me not to go insane from everything that happened was to form a kind of new me and at the same time preserve the old me inside myself. I couldn't be both at the same time. When I was adopted, when I came to Sweden, there was no one who could show me the way or help me process everything that had happened to me on the streets and in the orphanage. I wasn't ready to share that with my new parents or friends. Life had given us experiences that were far too different for me to dare to reveal my soul to them.

One day, the matron summoned me to her office. I was afraid that I'd done something wrong, something that had made her angry. On my way there, I tried to come up with a list of things I'd done wrong, but I couldn't think of a single one. When I stepped into the room, I was polite but on my guard. The matron smiled and asked me to come in and sit down in the brown chair in front of her desk. I relaxed a little. If I'd done something wrong or she was angry with me, she wouldn't have been so nice.

She started chatting about life at the orphanage, about how it was hard for children who grew up in an orphanage to be successful in life. She chatted about life on the streets and how hard that was. She was fishing for me to confirm that I understood what she was saying, so I nodded and murmured my agreement to all of it. That seemed to please her. I thought it was strange that we were having this weird little chat. She usually only summoned me to her office when I'd done something stupid or been extra nice and helpful. But here she was, chatting away. She was talking to me as if I were a grown-up, as if I were someone else and not one of the kids from the orphanage at all. She took out a white photo album. I'd never seen a photo album before, but I knew what photos were, and this album looked surprisingly thick. Before she let me look at the album, the matron asked me if I would want to leave the orphanage someday. I said yes, without even thinking about it or hesitating, and slightly too enthusiastically. I didn't want to leave the orphanage because it was a bad place. It was a thousand times better than life on the streets. And even though there were sometimes arguments or trouble between us kids, I have an astounding number of funny, happy memories of my time there. But for me, leaving the orphanage would mean that I would get to be with Mamãe. I missed her so much. The matron smiled and looked pleased. She told me to open the photo album. She came around from behind her desk and pulled up a chair so she could sit beside me while we looked at the pictures. On the front of the album, it said *Fotoalbum* along with several weird, long words. The matron told me it was written in a language called Swedish, that Sweden was a country far, far away. People spoke a different language there, and a lot of other things were different. I asked her if Sweden was like a place in a fairy tale. She gave me an odd look; then she smiled warmly at me and said that Sweden was like a place in a fairy tale. I liked fairy tales.

"Is Sweden a good fairy-tale place?" I asked the matron.

"I would say that it is," she replied.

"Are there magical creatures there?"

"There are many different animals there that we don't have here in Brazil," she replied.

"Are the animals there nice?"

"Just as nice as they are here in Brazil."

"But all the animals here aren't nice!"

"And they're not in Sweden, either," she replied, amused.

I liked the matron when she was nice and jovial like this.

"Do you want to go to Sweden?" she asked me.

I contemplated that for a moment. I'd always wanted to travel to one of Camile's fairy-tale lands and get to experience all the new and exciting things. Maybe I could be a princess in Sweden, and wear a long, white frilly gown, a crown on my head, and beautiful white shoes with heels. Maybe I could eat large amounts of candy. Surely Mamãe and Patrique would like this fairy-tale land of Sweden. Sweden might be the best fairy-tale land, and I was going to get to go there.

"Yes, I want to go to Sweden! But how do I get there?" I asked.

"On an airplane," the matron replied.

An airplane?! I thought. Wow, how luxurious! Only rich people got to travel in those big metallic birds that flew back and forth in the sky.

"Are the other children in the orphanage going to Sweden, too?" I asked.

"No, Christiana, only you. And there's one more thing I want to ask you: Do you want your little brother to go with you?"

What a stupid question. Of course I wanted Patrique to go, too! I would never leave him, not for anything.

"I'm not going anywhere without Patrique!" I said firmly.

The matron smiled and replied that she had suspected I would say as much. She asked me to open the photo album and look at the pictures. Before I opened it, I saw that at the bottom in the middle there was a bunny rabbit. It was a little comical. I wondered if someone had drawn it there just for me, because my last name was Coelho, which means rabbit in Portuguese. The rabbit looked happy. I wondered if they had rabbits in Sweden. I opened the album, and there were so many pictures inside. I saw a white lady and a white man standing in different places in the house and the yard, and everything looked very strange. I saw a bunch of little slips of white paper with black writing in Portuguese. I started reading what they said:

Sture na cozinha (Sture in the kitchen)

Sture no nosso quarto (Sture in our bedroom)

Lili-ann ocupada no nosso escritório (Lili-ann busy in our office)

Lili-ann jogando badminton no jardim com Sture (Lili-ann playing badminton in the yard with Sture)

And it continued like that throughout the entire photo album. I thought it was a little odd that they were just standing there and smiling in all these different nice rooms in the pictures. But maybe that was the kind of thing rich white people did? The matron started pointing to the pictures and explaining.

"Christiana, this is going to be your new home." She pointed to a picture of a red house with white trim around the windows. It looked like a nice house; there was a lot of grass around the house, and the grass was cut short. Only rich people had nice grass. In another picture, I saw a white room with white furniture, pink curtains, and a pink bedspread on the bed. I flipped to the next page in the album. I was astonished by what I saw: a big white bed with stuffed animals and a doll on it. The white lady, Lili-ann, was sitting on the bed, looking happy. There was a canopy over the bed. I had always wanted a canopy bed. Was I going to get my own canopy bed? That sounded too good to be true.

"Is this my bed?" I asked the matron, pointing at the picture in front of me.

"Yes, Christiana, it is. Do you like it?" she asked, smiling.

"I love it! Is it mine for sure?" I asked, feeling very skeptical. I'd learned on the streets that nothing is free.

"It's yours, along with everything else you see in the pictures," she said.

Something was wrong.

"Why would Patrique and I get to travel to the fairy-tale land of Sweden?" I asked.

"Because I want things to improve for you. I want you to have all the nice things you see in these pictures. Don't you like it?" she asked, and I felt like I must sound ungrateful.

"I really like it a lot!" I told her with a smile.

The truth was that I really, really, really liked it. I would get to fly in an airplane, travel to the fairy-tale country called Sweden, and I would have the most beautiful bed, eat candy, and get toys. There were a lot of rooms in my future house, and there were happy bunny rabbits there. What child wouldn't like that? The matron stood up. She said that I could take the album with me and show my friends, that it was mine now and that I should take good care of it.

"Are you sure my friends can't come to Sweden with me, just for a little while? Patricia could come, couldn't she?" I asked.

"If you could all go, Christiana, I would definitely send you all! Be happy now for this opportunity. Make the most of it. You can be whatever you want in Sweden. You could be a lawyer, a doctor, whatever you want. You'll have an opportunity that many children would love to get. You and your brother will be happy there, and you'll have two people who will take care of you and who will care about you very much. Aren't you glad?" she asked, and her eyes and body language warned me not to say anything other than yes.

"Yeah!" I said with a smile.

It didn't take long for the children at the orphanage to find out that my brother and I were going to be adopted, that we had gotten a family. This, getting a family, was always a big topic of conversation among the children. Many of them were orphans, and the dream of receiving love and warmth from a grown-up was strong. We all wanted our own rooms with toys and candy, to get to go to school and come back to a proper home. The other children were jealous that we'd been picked, and I liked that, liked the feeling that I was going to get something that everyone coveted.

Like all the other children in the orphanage, I had dreamed of living in a house. But I never had any doubt about where my home was. My home was wherever Mamãe was, near her and her warmth. I had also learned early on that you could dream and fantasize, but that reality was something completely different. Life was what it was, and it was no use spending much time thinking about it when you were eight years old and taking things one day at a time. Some days were fun and happy; others were painful or boring. But I started noticing how the other children whispered about me and peeked over at me with more and more loathing. I knew they were jealous. I knew it was just a matter of time before some of the kids took action.

It was always like this at the orphanage. We had so much fun together, all of us kids, but there was always a flip side. I tried to show that I wasn't afraid of them, which mostly I wasn't. I was afraid of them feeling sorry for me and pitying me, because I didn't want anyone to see me as weak. After I'd found out that my brother and I were going to be adopted, I was walking down the upstairs hallway in the orphanage, near the showers. That was when it happened.

Four or five kids from Gabriela's clique pulled me into the showers and started hitting and kicking me. I fought as hard as I could, hurled myself on one of the girls, and got her down onto the floor. Before I was able to punch her, the other kids were on top of me. I didn't stand a chance, and I knew that the more I fought, the harder they would wail on me. I'd learned on the streets that sometimes you had to take the pain, swallow your pride, and accept: *It's going to hurt, but they're not going to kill me.* And if they did kill me, boy, would they get an incredible beating. I got into a fetal position, curled up as much as I could, and let the kids kick and hit me. I tried to protect my head. I don't know how long it went on for. I just know that somewhere in the back of my mind, I thought I deserved it. It was the least I could endure for having let down my mother. I deserved pain. The pain would pass; what I'd done, though, that would never pass.

I don't know if I came around when the beating ended, or if I lay there on the cold floor for a long time. I only know that my body hurt, but not as much as my heart. I had been given preferential treatment, and for that I had to be punished. That's how life worked at the orphanage. I don't remember how I got up or where I went. I only know that I found Patricia, who knew right away what had happened. She asked how I was, and I said, "OK." I didn't need to say any more than that. If anyone could understand, she could. Whenever I was sad, Patricia was always there, and whenever she took a beating, I was always there for her. It didn't matter if I was physically there when it happened. I would always go search out the guilty party and give them payback. I wish that I could say that I always won and that the children stopped attacking her, but the truth was that I lost more fights than I won. And they came after me more than if I hadn't avenged her. But it was a matter of principle.

When it was time for dinner, Patricia stood up and held out her hand. I took it and tried to get up. I was in pain. Patricia said she was going to go get help; I quickly got up and said that wasn't necessary. She went for help anyway. She knew what would happen if she told, but she still went. I let her go. I know I would have done the same for her. The only difference was that I could stand up for myself so much better than she could. And now I was going to be leaving the orphanage, and Patricia was going to get beaten up because of me. It was her final gift to me. I know that she knew that I was going to pull through, but by going to get help, she gave me her friendship forever. That was her way of showing it, and I understood, so I let her go. I was eight years old and understood that pain can be beautiful, that it can be brave. I was already injured and Patricia knew that, but it wasn't the external wounds she wanted to take care of; it was my internal ones. Treating them required friendship, thoughtfulness, and love.

After Patricia, there was no one who looked after these wounds, no one I let get close enough, not for a very long time. Everyone who meant anything to me, everyone I loved, disappeared from my life.

The decision I'd made, at the age of eight, was not to let people into my life, not to love them from my heart. The pain when they went away or were taken from me was too immense.

Our Final Day at the Orphanage

The matron explained to me that the next morning, the two white people from the photo album were going to pick me up from the orphanage. They would take me home with them. My brother would come, too. A little later in the day, I got to meet them. It was both exciting and strange. They had weird names and expensive clothes. The matron had told me to be on my best behavior, to smile, to look happy. And I did as she asked. She had said that things would be so much better for me from now on and that I should be very grateful. Many children would have loved to trade places with me, she explained. She was right. Many of the children at the orphanage who didn't have parents had openly expressed their jealousy. They didn't understand that I didn't want to go anywhere, that I already had a mother. I hadn't understood that I was going to go away and become someone's new daughter. I didn't want a new home! I might have said yes to the adoption, but I had never asked for it. I didn't even know what the word *adoption* meant, not really.

One time I asked Mamãe if I could become rich, because then I could take care of her and my brother. She said that nothing was impossible, that the world is special, God is special, and that miracles can happen if you really wish for something. If you fight for it, anything can happen. So, I wished to become rich, as rich as white people.

The matron had asked me to smile and I smiled, but inside I was screaming and crying. I wasn't brave enough to contradict her. I was too much of a coward. We, all the children in the orphanage, respected her and were a little scared of her. She was nice to me, but at the same time she was stern. I never knew where I stood with her and, thank goodness, I rarely saw her. I would never say that she was cruel; I didn't believe that. I understood that she wanted to be kind, give me an opportunity, and give me a life. She had selected my brother and me, when she could have picked someone else. But she had done it without listening to me, without considering my emotions, and without really explaining. But I was eight years old, a child, and as an adult, it's easy to believe that you know more than a child even when it comes to their own feelings.

How could I have said no? What choice did I have? The matron could certainly never imagine the price I would pay, that over the course of my life, I would lose bits of my soul and not feel whole. I would become Christiana and Christina, without really knowing who I was. Is that a price worth paying for escaping extreme poverty? Yes, it is! But that doesn't make anything easier or better. There is a part of me that didn't want to say no to everything a child could desire. I didn't want to be poor anymore.

Within this long span of minutes in her office, which amounted to maybe a half hour, merely a few moments out of a single day, I had said yes to being adopted, to getting a new mother and father, to my brother getting to join me, and to traveling to the fairy-tale land of Sweden. There, the two white people would care for us and be nice. What I forgot to ask in all my eagerness was, Will Mamãe be going to Sweden, too? Who knows, maybe there was some significance to my forgetting to ask that question right then, and there was definitely a reason the matron didn't bring it up. Without my understanding what had really happened, my world had just started to turn upside down in a way that I could never have suspected.

That night, my last night in the orphanage, I didn't sleep at all. So many nights I had lain in my bed in the orphanage, the first bed I'd ever had, and stared at the ceiling, missing my mother. Now, bigger changes were afoot. I still didn't understand what they would entail. But I realized that I'd made a mistake, that I'd let my mother, my brother, and myself down. Everything that was going to happen the next day was my fault. My brother was asleep with the other babies in another part of the orphanage. He didn't know what I'd done. He didn't know the decision I'd made for us. I didn't know what the consequences of my decision would be, but I already had a bad feeling in the pit of my stomach. And I was afraid, so afraid. Everything felt surreal, and I had a hard time distinguishing between nightmares, daydreams, and reality. That night, I thought about a lot of things, and I cried. I knew that crying wouldn't help, because no one saw my tears, and even if someone did, there wasn't anyone to care, anyway. No one besides my friend Patricia and Mamãe. Mamãe was out there somewhere, wondering why she wasn't allowed to see me, wondering how I was doing, missing me. She loved me, and there she was, somewhere out there, surely close to the orphanage, with no idea that I would soon disappear to a place she couldn't follow me to. I cried the way my mother used to cry, silently and alone. One single string of words kept running through my head: *Mamãe, are you there? I've ruined everything. Can you hear me? Please answer. I'm sorry!*

I lay there, thinking about God. I thought about my fledgling bird from the cave and wondered whether it had found any friends. I wondered whether the angels saw me and whether God was there by my side. I thought about all the children who would be staying at the orphanage. What would happen to them? What would happen to Patricia? Would we see each other again, or would she, too, be one of the people who only existed in my heart? I looked over at her. She was asleep. Tomorrow, something was going to happen, and I had no way of knowing that what was waiting around the corner would shock me.

Out of nowhere, a new day dawned, and I wasn't even tired. I should have been completely exhausted after so much fear and so little sleep, after my brain had worked on overdrive all night. But I was alert. And since today was special, I didn't need to stand in the shower line. One of the employees had been assigned to look after me and make me look nice, so I got to bypass the whole line. I saw Patricia standing toward the very back. There was a pang in my heart. I didn't know if anyone would look after her once I was no longer around. I worried about her, but I didn't dare ask any of the other girls to take care of Patricia. I was scared that Patricia would be punished after I left the orphanage. I walked past the line, and everyone stared at me. I averted my gaze and walked right into the shower. The other children had to wait until I was done. Today I thoroughly washed. They gave me soap and some kind of sponge to really scrub myself clean. They'd already gone through my hair a few days earlier to remove the lice. They gave me a shampoo that smelled like fruit, and I massaged it into my hair.

When I was done, I dried myself thoroughly and was given a pair of underpants to put on. I could see that they weren't the usual underpants we kids normally wore. These were a little nicer, a little newer. I put them on and passed the kids again on my way out. I noted that one of the girls had helped Patricia move farther up in the line. I was suddenly so grateful that I had shared some of my Bon O Bon chocolates specifically with her. Our eyes met. She gave me a little smile, and I smiled back in gratitude. This was a wonderful gift she gave me, and I was certain that she knew it. I stopped, and the woman who had been helping me put her hand on my back and started pushing me forward. I looked up at her and asked her to wait. She did; maybe she'd seen something in my eyes that she understood, because usually they didn't care what we kids thought. I turned and looked at Patricia. This was the last time we would see each other. I wanted to go over to her and hug her, but I didn't want to make her vulnerable. Most of all, I probably couldn't have handled it. So, I smiled at her, and she smiled back and raised her hand to give me the Brazilian *figa* gesture, which is to say that she made a fist but with her thumb up between her index finger and her middle finger to wish me good luck. I returned the gesture. I thought I would see Patricia one more time and get to say goodbye, but I never saw her again. I hadn't even given her a hug, which I still regret to this day.

The woman helped me get dressed. I put on my chicken-yellow sweatpants and a matching long-sleeved sweatshirt. I was given white socks and white shoes; they were a little too small for my feet and unbelievably uncomfortable. A hair-pick comb was produced, and the woman used it to fluff up my hair. I didn't like it. I brushed my teeth with real toothpaste, and then the woman and I started walking down the hallway, down the stairs, and through the next hallway that went by the gate that was the entrance to the orphanage. I peeked out, hoping for a glimpse of my mother. I didn't see her. We kept moving down the hallway and stepped into the matron's office. She thanked the orphanage employee who'd been with me all morning and asked her to leave us.

I could feel my heart beating so hard inside my rib cage that I was forced to look down and check whether it was visible from the outside. As I stood there, the matron chatted away. I knew I ought to listen, but I couldn't focus. Then the door opened, and a woman walked in, holding Patrique in her arms. He didn't look very happy, either. He wasn't crying, but he did not look pleased. The matron asked me to have a seat, and I sat on a brown chair against the wall. She explained how great everything was going to be for me, how important it was that I be nice, and she told me to smile when the people came to pick me up. I nodded but couldn't get a single word out. For the first time, I saw something in the matron's eyes that gave me hope. She looked a little worried, a little anxious, and maybe even a little scared. I hoped she was going to change her mind, that she was going to realize this was all a big mistake, but I knew better. What had I learned on the streets? You could dream and you could fantasize, but you always had to separate those dreams and fantasies from reality. Reality was anything but a dream.

146

Suddenly, there was a knock on the door. In stepped two people I had met for the first time the day before. They smiled and looked happy, but also a little tense. There was some talking among the adults, and someone asked me to say hello, which I did. The woman who had been holding Patrique handed him over to the lady, who was clearly going to be our new mother. She smiled and carefully took him into her arms. The instant she took him, Patrique started to cry. Big tears rolled down his cheeks. He reached out his hands to the woman who'd handed him over. Everything inside me ached. I wanted to run over, take him into my arms, and reassure him that everything was OK, that I was there. But I stood silently in my place like a good little girl. The matron asked me to walk over and hug my new mother and father. I walked over and hugged them.

The matron took a picture of all of us together, and I stood there and smiled as I had been ordered to do. After what could have been five minutes or five hours, it was time to go. We all walked to the gate: my new mother and father, me, Patrique, the matron, and two other orphanage women, two that I liked. Our new mother held Patrique, who had now stopped crying and had started pulling on her hair and glasses instead, but not in the way I would have liked, more out of curiosity. The gate opened, and my new father took my hand. It felt incredibly weird. I could fend for myself, had always done so, and I didn't need someone—definitely not a stranger—to hold my hand. We stepped out the gate and started walking down the sidewalk, away from the orphanage. I turned around and saw the three orphanage women wave and smile at me. I felt something that was worse than just about anything I'd felt before. I felt a dreadful panic. I felt terror. Reality had caught up with me. I could no longer pretend that everything would miraculously work out and that everything would feel better. I tried to pull free from the man's—my new father's—grasp. I screamed and cried. Struggling to get free, I screamed to the matron that I didn't want to go, that I would be nicer, that I would help out more. I could see that she was uneasy, but not enough to do anything about it. The man pulled on my arm. The matron called out that everything would be fine, gave me one final wave, walked back onto the orphanage grounds, and closed the gate behind her. There was no use screaming anymore or resisting. I turned around and went with them, my new parents. I felt all my security draining away. I was lost and grief-stricken. I felt all alone in the world, which felt overwhelmingly big. What could little me do? My new father held my hand. As I walked, every now and then, my new mother would peek down at me worriedly. But I just walked, numbed and exhausted. We got into a taxi that was waiting by the orphanage. I cried and cried, I wasn't strong enough for this . . . I didn't think there was any way to hurt me more. Physically, there was no longer any pain I couldn't bear. Anyone who needs to survive on the streets must learn how to withstand unbearable pain, if only to maintain their pride in situations where they know they don't stand a chance and have no hope. I was scared, but I brought a part of me, behind my wall of pride, into the unknown and to a new world.

No one was going to see how scared I was, and I was scared out of my wits!

Visit to the Orphanage
2015

I have no concept of how long Rivia and I have been waiting outside the orphanage for them to come out and let us in. I realize I'm still clutching the gate when a boy of about seven comes out and looks at us curiously. I greet him, and he greets me back. We're let in through the gate and instructed to wait just inside it. I look around, and everything is surreal. On the verge of tears, I step back over to the gate. I glance at Rivia, who smiles lovingly and warily asks me how I'm feeling. I tell her about the gate and my mother. I'm not sad as I'm telling her about it. I realize that time has done what I had never believed possible: it has healed this wound, at least a bit.

Now, as I stand here once again, instead of feeling anger, I feel love. Those painful memories of being ripped away from my mother will never go away. I don't want them to. They're a part of me, they shaped me, but I'm capable of seeing a completely different bigger picture now, to really see it. Over the years, I've had people tell me that I should feel grateful for getting a chance at a better life, and it has really irritated me. We humans have a strong tendency to universalize our own opinions, thoughts, and feelings and assume they apply to other people. No one but me knows what I feel and what I've been through. And it's really not up to anyone else to say what I should and shouldn't feel. Of course, I'm grateful that I escaped from the squalor of the slums and got a chance to get an education, to work, and to live in a social democracy. But there are so many other things in life that have meaning besides the job title on my business card, the car I drive, or how many pairs of designer jeans I own. As I stand here at this gate, which feels so much smaller than when I was eight, I'm grateful, unbelievably grateful, not because I have a car, a nice apartment, and a bunch of stuff. I'm grateful for something completely different. I realize that I already pulled the biggest winning ticket long ago: I got to live. Neither Camile nor the boy by the trash cans got that chance. I received a new life with a chance to fulfill myself, something so many children dream of but never receive. Yes, it's been tough, and there have been times I thought I would go insane, or when I just wanted to disappear, but there have been love, friendship, family, and fantastic, amazing people in my life. How could I stand here today and feel anything but an overwhelming love and joy?

I have Rivia here with me, and soon I will get answers to my questions. What actually happened when I was adopted? Why did it happen so fast, and why weren't my mother and I allowed to see each other? I've wondered about this my whole life. I've struggled, I've carried these painful experiences with me, and I have lived with this absence. None of this has disappeared or changed as I stand here now at the very gate that separated me from my mother and my security. I'm still carrying this. But the same thing that happened to my memory of seeing the devil dancing in the streets of Diamantina—I later came to understand that it was Carnival and people were wearing costumes—happens to these memories now. They're the same, and it still hurts to remember them, but I have a different understanding and another way of relating to them now. Instead of seeing what I've lost, what was taken away from me, and all the injustices that were done to me, I can see the power of what I've received. And I've created it myself. Throughout my life, I have made the choice to never see myself as a victim. As I stand here at this yellow gate, which I have associated with pain for years, I realize that my life really hasn't been about finding myself, but about creating myself.

I'm standing here thinking all this when a skinny, energetic woman who looks about forty-five or fifty approaches us with a big smile. She looks at me and says my name, Christiana, and then she hugs me. There's something very familiar about her, but I can't place her. She smells like a mixture of perfume and cigarettes. She introduces herself as Igelausia and explains that she's the matron of the orphanage. We stand out by the gate for a bit chatting, with Rivia translating. Igelausia says that she worked in the orphanage when I lived there. Suddenly, I picture a beautiful young woman in front of me, and I realize now why she seemed so familiar. She invites us in, and we enter the building.

The first thing I encounter is an enormous mosaic of Jesus. I'm fascinated at how something that was completely absent from my memory for twenty-four years can suddenly be there again. I even remember the details of the Jesus picture when I see it. I have a memory of standing in front of it as a little girl and puzzling over why Jesus was so white.

Igelausia leads us to her office, where she sits down at her desk and I sit across from her. I look around and realize the chairs are the same ones from my era and that the metal filing cabinet is still there. Igelausia takes out a little present, which she hands to me. I accept it, thanking her, and I feel guilty that I didn't think to buy anything for her. When I unwrap it, I'm holding a little red jewelry box in my hand. I open it and see a beautiful piece of jewelry. It's the Virgin Mary, and I say to myself that I'll buy a pretty chain for the charm when I get home to Sweden. I thank her and say that it's so beautiful and that she didn't need to get me anything.

Then she takes out a photograph and hands it to me. She keeps talking, very rapidly, her words coming out while she breathes in and out. I recognize the rhythm and the speed, just like how I speak when I'm excited about something or happy or irritated. The picture was taken in 1991, and I see myself, my little brother, and Igelausia out behind the orphanage. From somewhere, I hear Rivia explain that Igelausia says she saved this picture for all these years because she knew that one day I would come back. I turn the picture over and see that something is written on the back: Patrick's and my Brazilian names and the date when it was taken. I turn the picture over again and realize that I'm looking at the youngest Christina I've ever seen or, well, Christiana. I have no pictures of myself from before the age of eight. I've always been a little sad not knowing what I looked like when I was little. Whenever I've looked through my friends' photo albums, I've always felt a little jealous that they do know. I've thought that when I have children, I won't know whether they look like me when I was little.

Igelausia asks about Patrick—Patrique—and how he's doing. She proceeds to fill me in on what's happened at the orphanage since we left. She says that the building I'm in now, which was my old childhood home, serves as a combined preschool and childcare center now, both for the children from the orphanage and for other neighborhood children. The parents drop off and pick up their kids here. She says that the new orphanage is a few blocks away and that later on we'll walk over there and say hello. She says that the laws have changed in Brazil, and orphanages aren't allowed to house as many children as they did back in my day. She says that when I lived here, there were almost two hundred children in the orphanage, but that now any one orphanage is allowed to house only twenty children. I smile a little. It feels good to know that I can rely on my memory. She also says that people now try to place the children with members of their own families. If that doesn't work, then it's foster care, and if that doesn't work, adoption is the last alternative.

She also says that what happened to my brother and me in 1991 couldn't happen today. I look at her and realize that she knows what happened. I don't think she would have said that if she thought everything had happened the way it should. I glance at Rivia and then have her ask Igelausia what actually happened when we were adopted.

Igelausia looks a little more serious now as she talks. My mother came to visit the orphanage with me and Patrique. The orphanage offered to take Patrique and help him, since he was so little and also sick. A month later, they also took me. The people working at the orphanage noticed that everything wasn't right with my mother. They doubted her ability to take care of her children. When they found out that she had two other sons whom she hadn't been able to care for, and that that case had gone through the courts, they felt that she was not capable of raising two more children. To save time, instead of filing two separate cases, the courts decided to combine both cases, the one for my two older brothers and the one for me and my little brother. The orphanage knew that it was hard to find adoption placements for older children, so it wanted a quick ruling. My mother didn't show up for the appointed court date, and that was how she lost custody of all her children. The court prohibited her from visiting me and my brother.

Igelausia explains what I already know: the court ruling didn't stop my mother from coming and standing outside the orphanage hollering until she got to see us. She said that as soon as they managed to arrange an adoption for me and Patrique, they needed to make sure we stopped seeing Mamãe, so it would be easier for us children to proceed. But Mamãe kept coming to the orphanage and shouting that she wanted to see us. She did that for a long time. Igelausia glances at me and says that she remembers how it embarrassed me and I found it tiresome. I just nod. She repeats that what happened to us could never happen today. Now, they get in touch with relatives and do everything they can to keep the child in the family. I don't know what to say to her. I'm not here to blame anyone for what happened. I know that their priority was looking after Patrique's and my health, and I feel now that this is all in the past. I'm glad to have her explain the whole thing and give me their perspective, but I also have my own perspective and am sure that my family has its own as well. I just wanted to know what had happened here at the orphanage, and now I do. She says that all the court documents are searchable and that she can help me do that. I say that I would really like that.

We leave her office to tour the orphanage. I ask Rivia to tell her that I want to try to navigate on my own, following my memories. We start by walking to the dining hall and the kitchen. I smile when I find them without any problem. I feel like a giant in a dollhouse, not because the building is small, because it really isn't, but because everything looks so little now compared to how I remember it from my childhood. The hallways seem narrower and shorter, and the tables in the dining hall look unbelievably tiny. We're in the room where I ate every day for a year, and I show Rivia where my seat used to be, all the way over by the exit. You never knew when you might need to make a quick exit.

From the dining hall, we move into the kitchen, where there's a platter of fruit on a metal table. Huge papayas, pineapples, and avocados. I take an avocado and hold it up to Rivia. But, oh my God, they're so big, just the way I remember them, not like the little ones we have in Sweden. I remember how I used to pick unripe avocados in the backyard and stash them in the fridge, how I charmed the food service ladies so they would let me do that, and in exchange, I helped them with the cooking in my spare time. I was street-smart, and I'm very aware of where those smarts came from: the fear of not knowing when I would eat again, the awareness that I had to take care of myself and try to think ahead and stockpile so there would be food for me in the future. I ask Rivia to take a picture of me with the gigantic avocado and laugh. If, when I was eight years old, someone had told me that one day I would come back to the orphanage after having lived in a distant land for twenty-four years and be overjoyed to hold a Brazilian avocado, I'm pretty sure I wouldn't have believed it.

Igelausia presents an older woman who works in the kitchen. She says that she used to work in the kitchen back when I lived in the orphanage, but I don't remember her like I remember Igelausia. Coffee and cookies are produced, and we sit down at a table in the middle of the kitchen.

After coffee, Rivia, Igelausia, and I stroll up a little hill to the new orphanage. Igelausia lights a cigarette, takes a puff, and continues talking about the new orphanage. Igelausia says that in 2004, it became illegal for any orphanage in Brazil to have more than twenty children, and they had two years to implement that. She continues by saying that in 2006, it was decided that orphanages should be designed so that the children would feel like they were living in a home and not an institution.

At the top of the hill, we turn left. Igelausia continues to smoke her cigarette. I think about what she's said. Back in my day, there were almost two hundred children living in the orphanage. What happened to all the children who didn't get to stay? We reach a black gate, and behind the gate I see a pretty brown building. It pleases me to see that the children live in a building that looks like a house. A woman meets us and opens the gate. I'm carrying the big box containing all the little boxes of chocolates, and I greet her with a smile. I feel myself starting to get a bit nervous. Soon I'm going to meet a bunch of children, children of all ages, children I know have been through terrible ordeals, children I know are going to have a hard time in life. What should I say to them? I take a deep breath and enter the building. Some kids who look like they're somewhere between ten and sixteen are sitting on a dark-colored sofa. They're watching TV. When I look more closely, I see that they're playing a video game. I smile, remembering how we used to watch *Xuxa* and *RoboCop* in my day; of course they're playing a video game now.

I set down the box with all the chocolates. Igelausia says something to the children. The kids pause the video game, and she explains to the kids who Rivia and I are. I hear how she says my name again, and all the children look at me. I can feel their eyes scrutinizing me from top to bottom. I smile and look them in the eyes. Rivia explains that

Igelausia just told the kids I used to live in the orphanage, that I had been adopted by a Swedish couple, and that now I was back to visit.

While Igelausia chats and Rivia translates, one of the boys from the group catches my interest a little more than the other kids. Something about his eyes, his body language, and the look on his face makes me think back to a little Christiana. I try to figure out what it is about the boy and realize that he's got street smarts, that he's a real street kid. I recognize it from where his eyes go, his smile, and how his brain is in overdrive.

It's my turn to introduce myself. Rivia translates. I tell them about myself and about what it was like at the orphanage when I lived here. I can see from their faces that they think I speak a funny-sounding language. When I say I've brought chocolates and ask if they want them, they nod eagerly. I start handing out the yellow boxes. I feel so much joy at doing this, but I also feel sad that this is all I have to give them. Some of the kids hug me, and with others I initiate a hug. The little boy gives me a big hug and immediately starts chatting with me. He asks about my language. He wonders why I don't speak Portuguese. I explain to him that in Sweden, people don't speak Portuguese, so I've forgotten how. He keeps asking me about everything conceivable, and a part of me feels like somehow I know this boy, even though obviously I don't.

I had asked Igelausia before if we could chat in a little more depth with some of the kids, the ones who want to. We walk into another room where a couple of girls are waiting. Natali is twelve and Lais is eleven. We form a little ring, Rivia, Natali, Lais, and I. Here I am, sitting with these two incredibly sweet girls, and what had at first seemed like such a good idea now doesn't feel right. I have no training when it comes to talking to kids who've experienced trauma. I'm not a psychologist. What if what I'm doing now is somehow harmful to the girls? How can I just ask them to give me something without giving anything back? I decide that I have something different from the knowledge education can give—I have experienced the world these girls grew up in. I brace myself for what I know will be an emotional time if the girls trust us and open up. I glance over at Rivia and tell her that what we're going to hear now will be heartrending and tough. I contemplate for a moment how I should say the next thing to her. Rivia is an unbelievably empathetic and thoughtful person, and she might start crying, which I know isn't what these children need. Rivia is going to be in a tough spot, because she has to translate. That means she's not only going to listen to what the girls have been through, but she's also going to have to retell it. I inform Rivia that no matter what the girls tell us, we cannot start crying. We can show that we sympathize with them, but if they don't cry, we absolutely cannot cry. I know that what I've just told her sounds heartless, but I'm thinking of what's best for the girls. Rivia and I can deal with our feelings about whatever we're going to hear later, but not in front of the girls. I realize that asking these children to trust a total stranger with their life stories and all the troubles they've been through is asking a lot. I decide that I must and that I want to give them a part of me, a part of my story.

I ask them if they want to hear my story, what I went through before I was adopted. They do. I start recounting, and the girls sit transfixed. When I tell them about my time in the favela, I see them nod knowingly. That makes me sad, because that means they've experienced the same pain. I know I don't need to elaborate to make what I'm saying real. They understand.

When I give lectures in Sweden, I try to paint a detailed picture for my audience so they can really understand what happened on the streets. When I tell these girls about Camile, my voice breaks, and Natali stretches out her little hand and puts it on mine for a brief moment. Natali is the first to ask questions, questions about my new home and country. I take out my phone and show them some pictures. The girls look, curious. I know what they're thinking, that they'll never have this life. It gets to me a little, and the thought that maybe I'm doing more harm than good pops into my mind again. They ask me whether I've thought about learning Portuguese, and whether I've ever thought about adopting a child. Natali asks me if I did adopt, would I adopt a baby or an older child. I respond that I would probably adopt an older child since most people just want to adopt younger children. I tell her that I was older when I was adopted and that I know what that means. She seems satisfied with my answer.

Natali starts telling her story first. She says she lived in the favela for five years, that her mother is poor, and what little money they had went for the alcohol her father drank. He was always drunk, and Natali had to take care of her siblings—two sisters and a brother. She describes how her father abused her mother and her siblings, how she tried to protect them but that it wasn't easy. Now her siblings have been adopted to Italy, and she misses them very much. They told her she was too old and that in Italy you couldn't adopt a child over a certain age, so she was left behind. She says that her brother is four and her sisters are seven and nine. She hopes she'll see them again but doesn't know if she will. I can see that it's hard for Natali to talk about this, but also that she's steeled herself for this discussion. A solitary tear runs down her cheek, and I feel like my heart is going to burst. I recognize that solitary tear so well. There's so much behind one of those tears, a river of pain, loss, and longing. I feel a tear run down my cheek, and it's my turn to stretch out my hand and hold hers. But it doesn't feel like enough, so I lean over and hug her. There's so much I want to give her, so much love, but I don't really know how. I want to say that it will be OK and that life will get better. But lying isn't the right way to go. She would know, and I would feel like a fraud. So, I let go and let her continue. She tells me that she misses her mother, that she thinks her mother abandoned them, because she hasn't seen her for many years. It occurs to me that her mother might not even be alive anymore, but I keep this thought to myself. She suddenly lights up and says that she's learning *capoeira* and that she's the only girl in the orphanage who is. She says that she loves hanging out and doesn't like making her bed. Rivia and I laugh, and I tell Natali that I'm not a big fan of bed making, either.

Now it's Lais's turn. The pretty young girl with short hair and glasses glances at me and Rivia, and smiles a bit modestly. She's the shy one. You can hear it in her voice and see it in her body language. Her hands rest on her thighs, and her fingers are interlaced. She takes a deep breath and explains that she lived with her mother, who couldn't take care of her and her siblings. She says that her mother worked long hours at a shopping mall and was almost never home. Her stepfather, whom she lived with, beat her and her seven siblings. She tells us that she loves all her siblings and that she knows who they all are, except for the youngest one. Lais says that she lived with her biological father for a while, but he used a lot of drugs, so she had to go back to her mother. She explains that her stepfather wound up in jail, but her mother helped him get out. Her mother often got home from work around midnight, so Lais had to take care of her siblings. When she told her mother that her stepfather hit her and her siblings, her mother didn't believe her. Lais looks sad and glances down at her hands. She says that she thinks it's strange that her mother didn't believe her. That's what her life was like until she was eight, when a social worker came and got her. Lais says that she likes it here at the orphanage, and she likes the other kids. When I ask her what she hopes for, she says that she really wants to see her youngest sibling, her sister. "I'd like to see her at least once," she says. When I ask what she wants to be when she grows up, she smiles and says a ballerina.

The Fairy-Tale Land of Sweden
1991

It was midsummer when I first arrived at my new home in Sweden, a red house with a "No. 6" by the door, with white trim and a brown fence around the whole yard. I remember that even though I had been completely devastated by my departure from the orphanage, I had started to accept the change after the five weeks in Brazil I spent with my new parents, Lili-ann and Sture, while everything was finalized for our departure to Sweden. However, I still hadn't fully understood what had happened. I think there's a limit to how much pain and sadness a person can handle at one time. I would be lying if I said that I was sad when I saw the house. After all, I'd never had a real home before. This was my and Patrique's—or *Patrick* as he would be called now—new home, and my curiosity took over.

I walked into the house, and I can't describe the overwhelming emotion. We were rich! I was going to live with rich people. The first thing Lili-ann did was show me my room. I remember it as if it were yesterday, stepping into it for the first time. The wallpaper was white with a little pink and blue, and it wasn't smooth. It had little bumps that you could scrape off with your fingernails or with something sharp. Later, after I'd lived there for a while, I made patterns on the wallpaper by scraping away the little textured bumps. I had a white desk, white wardrobe cupboards, and on the far wall, my bed. It was an old-fashioned daybed that had a knob in the middle of the headboard. My first thought was that this couldn't be my room. I mean, I'd seen the picture in the photo album. My bed was bigger, and it looked fluffy and had a white comforter that went all the way down to the floor. In the middle of the ceiling over the bed was a canopy made of see-through fabric that shrouded the bed like a little house, and it had pretty, fluffy pillows. Nothing looked like it had in the picture. I tried to ask where my real bed was. Finally, I took out the photo album I had been given at the orphanage and showed Lili-ann the picture of the bed. I pointed to the picture and then to me. Lili-ann understood and shook her head and pointed to the bed in the room, and then to me. I didn't even try to hide my disappointment. My princess bed, which was one of the few things I had been looking forward to, had been faked. I'd been tricked. I felt stupid, but I was also angry. Like Camile had said, you couldn't trust white people.

When I later discovered that the bed that was supposed to have been mine was in the home of Lili-ann's friend and neighbor, Gunilla Sandström, my disillusionment did not help matters. It turned out to be Gunilla's daughter Lisa's. She was a year older than I was. *Of course,* I thought, *the princess bed belonged to a white girl.*

Lili-ann and Sture continued showing me around the house. The kitchen was unbelievably beautiful and massive. They showed me the living room, or the best room as it later came to be called, and I understood that they were careful with this room. I wasn't allowed to touch anything in there. It was a room that wasn't used very often. It was very nice, and if I'd had any doubt that my new parents were rich, those doubts vanished as soon as I saw the best room. We continued down the stairs and into the basement. Lili-ann carried Patrick for the whole tour. There was a big TV down there with some kind of device underneath it. In the middle of the room was an odd wooden machine. It had a zillion strings and colorful yarn on the strings, and it took up almost the entire room. I gave Lili-ann a quizzical look. She could tell I was curious and handed Patrick to Sture. I could see that he was growing more and more comfortable holding the baby. The last thing I wanted was for him to drop my brother on the floor. Mamãe would never forgive me. Lili-ann walked over to the wooden machine and explained that it was a *vävstol*, a loom. Why did these people have such weird, difficult words for everything? What was wrong with the words I knew? She showed me how you used the loom and asked if I wanted to try. I shook my head and backed away, which wasn't like me. I was a very curious person and liked trying new things, but I didn't want to give her the impression that she and I were friends. I already had a mother, and Lili-ann shouldn't think I'd forgotten that.

We went upstairs and into Lili-ann and Sture's bedroom. There were white walls, a white bed with a pink comforter, pink curtains for the big windows, and white wardrobe cupboards. The room was nice and made for an adult princess. We walked through the room and out onto the patio. The backyard was huge and the lawn enormous. There was a little glass house and a tree that looked prickly, and then a silver fir came into view. I'd never seen a tree like that before. Lili-ann and Sture led me across the lawn to the far side where Sture pointed to a big, white rectangular surface. I didn't know what it was, but it looked like a swimming pool. I pointed to it and then mimed a few swimming strokes with my arms. I didn't wait for Sture to confirm that I was right since we were rich and all rich families had a pool. I got a running start and was about to jump in when a couple of strong arms caught me around the middle and stopped me in midjump.

Sture pulled up the white covering, which was some kind of cloth, and then I saw that there were vegetables growing underneath it. He pulled up one of the plants, and there were tiny little brown tubers covered in dirt, dangling off the plant. It wasn't a swimming pool. It was a potato patch.

I'll never forget my first night in Sweden in my new bed. I remember that I was completely exhausted. It had been a long day with so many new impressions. I had mixed feelings. The new things were exciting, but also frightening. For every positive emotion I had, there was an opposing, negative emotion. Having so many emotions at the same time was overwhelming. Underlying it all there was a fear and a worry that ran deep into my soul.

That night, I brushed my teeth in our fancy new bathroom. I brushed my teeth with a pink toothbrush and Colgate toothpaste. Lili-ann had given me a white cotton nightgown with flowers all over it. It came down to my knees, and at first, I found it uncomfortable. Lili-ann had put my little brother to bed several hours earlier, and I'd looked in on him a couple of times. He was sleeping in a white crib in their room. I rinsed the toothpaste out of my mouth and washed my face, apparently something you were supposed to do before you went to bed. Lili-ann and Sture came into the room and tucked me in, and I smiled to be nice, smiled to show my appreciation and gratitude. But I felt like I was letting these people do things I was not at all comfortable with. It felt like they were taking liberties that I hadn't granted them. But that was how life was and had always been. People took what they wanted, and sometimes you had to accept it.

Lili-ann wanted to lead me in a prayer, and she expected me to clasp my hands and fingers together. But that was not how we prayed in Brazil, and if there was one thing I had no intention of doing, it was praying the wrong way. So, I held my hands the way we did in Brazil, the way I did with my real mother, with my palms flat together and my fingers pointed up. Lili-ann started praying slowly in Swedish: *God, who loves the children dear, look after me so young in years . . .*

It was an odd prayer. I didn't understand much of it, but I could hear the rhythm in what she was saying, and it had the rhythm of a prayer. Lili-ann and Sture said good night and turned off the light, but they left the door ajar, and I noticed that the hallway light was still on. After they left the room, I sat up cross-legged in bed. I brought my hands together and let my fingers point up at the ceiling. I leaned my head down a little toward my ribs, and I started praying, but not the new prayer. I was my real mother's daughter, and I might perform outwardly for my new parents and do what they wanted, but here in solitude where no one else owned me, I prayed: *Santa Maria, cheia de graça, o senhor é convosco.*

This was the prayer my mother and I used to pray. I sat there, my legs crossed, tears streaming down my cheeks. My tears always burned, and it felt like I had gravel in my eyes. I was so tired, so done! I heard Mamãe's voice in my head: *Christiana, lie down and go to sleep! Everything will feel better when you wake up.*

That night, I dreamed that I woke up in a big room that was light blue and looked fluffy. I discovered that the room was a cloud. Something behind me was glowing brightly and providing a warm light. I turned around and must have been looking at the sun, because the light was so bright, it hurt even to just glance at it. I covered my eyes and tried to figure out where the heck I was. My body felt warm and wonderful. I felt safe and loved. There was so much warmth and affection in the room. I must be with the cloud people. *Camile, are you here?* As soon as I asked my question, I heard the answer. *No, Christiana, she isn't in this room!* The voice was warm and soft, but still imposing. I immediately knew that the speaker was someone I should respect, not be afraid of, but also not annoy. *Where am I?* I asked a bit hesitantly. As I asked the question, I knew the answer. *You know where you are, and you know who I am.* I saw a big throne, and I realized the figures around me I thought were people were angels. I looked at them and smiled, but they just looked at me, neither angry nor happy. I knew that I shouldn't look up at whoever was sitting on the throne. Every cell and fiber of my being told me that I shouldn't look up. But as curious as I always am and was, of course I looked up. I remember the power of the emotion: I was looking at God. God sat on the big throne. I immediately fell to my knees and made the sign of the cross over my face and chest, but the instant I did that, I knew I had ruined everything. I hadn't received permission to look at God. I knew that, but I had done it anyway. I felt the atmosphere in the room change, and the sense of displeasure was strong. It was pressing in on me, and I could feel how it pushed on my body and penetrated all the way into my heart.

Christiana? Do you know why you're here? You're here because you made a mistake. You're here because you made too many mistakes.

I'm sorry, please, forgive me! Tell me what I need to do to fix it, to be good! Please!

You haven't followed your heart. You haven't followed what you know to be right. And you won't get to come to heaven and to me again until you do.

Suddenly, the floor I was standing on turned into a cloud. I began to fall and looked up in fear at God and the angels, but they were gone. I had time only to cry out for help before I plunged completely through the clouds. I fell and fell. It was terrifying. I fell belly down, past planets, suns, galaxies. It was so beautiful, but the horrible feeling of falling was so palpable. I was so scared. I fell toward the Milky Way and toward our solar system. I passed planet after planet, until I saw the earth. I fell toward it, fell through the atmosphere, and then I was surrounded by fire. I fell toward Sweden. I saw our house in Vindeln, and I fell toward it. I was panic-stricken. God had banished me, and I was going to crash and die. I saw the house coming closer and closer. My panic and fear grew. The house was so close now. I screamed with all my might, and just as my body smashed into the roof, a hand seemed to turn me over in the air, and I fell through the roof, back first. I can't describe the pain. I felt my spine snap in two. My ribs were dashed to pieces. I felt wood skewering into my back. I screamed as I fell, and just before I hit the bed, I woke up, sitting upright in bed and screaming.

Lili-ann came running into the room. She ran over to the bed and sat down on the edge and asked what had happened. She looked terrified. I was in so much pain and couldn't stop screaming. I felt the pain start to abate, but it still hurt. I screamed and cried, and she held me. I let her hold me. I was already lost anyway. What was it God had said? *Christiana, you have disappointed me.* He had said that I couldn't come back to heaven. My new mother could hold me, but I was lost and unloved by the one who was supposed to love everyone. God didn't love me. I calmed down after a while, and I pushed her away gently. I didn't want her to feel like she wasn't wanted. I really knew what that felt like. I lay back down in bed, and she tucked me in.

I've tried many times to analyze what this dream meant. After everything I'd been through up to that night, after all the new things I'd seen and experienced, after all the emotional storms and all the being lost, after I'd been ripped away from my security and my roots, I accused myself of so much. Children take so much blame upon themselves, and I couldn't forgive myself. But for me, it's not just that. My mother talked so much about God and angels, and I had heard so many wonderful stories when I was little. Since then, I've always wanted to believe that there was something magical in our world and that not everything was logical and rational. Isn't it a miracle that of all the children who could be adopted, who deserved it more than me, and who had been in the orphanage significantly longer than I had, it was my brother and I who received this chance at a better life?

But back then, I had a long way to go before I could see that.

I prayed quietly to myself that night, before I fell asleep again. I whispered it so my new mother could hear it. I didn't care. She wouldn't understand what I said anyway, and if she did, then I didn't care. I prayed one last time, and then it was over. God had abandoned me, so why shouldn't I abandon God?

I woke up the next morning feeling like something had snapped inside me. I was broken. I thought I'd already felt everything a person could feel, but apparently it could get worse. Luckily, I didn't know then that emotionally, things were only going to get tougher.

My new mother yelled that breakfast was ready, so I went to the kitchen in my white nightgown. The first twenty-four hours had passed, and I had survived, just barely. But I had survived. It was a really good breakfast. Lili-ann had made oatmeal. At first, I was skeptical. It looked like sludgy pale mud, and I remember that I gave her a look as if to say, *Are you trying to poison me?* Sture and Patrick were sitting at the table, too, and Sture had already eaten his sludge, so I assumed it was edible. I added sugar and poured milk on top. There were hardboiled eggs on the table, and I loved those. There were also ham, cheese, sliced tomatoes and pickles, jam, bananas, and a tube of something. The tube was blue with a blond boy's face on it. I watched Lili-ann and Sture squeeze the contents of the tube onto their eggs. Lili-ann asked if I wanted some, and I smiled and said yes. If there was one thing I didn't turn down, it was food. Lili-ann said it was smoked cod roe, and I took a dollop of it with my finger and tasted it. It was disgusting! I spit it out, took the water glass that was in front of me, and drank big, greedy gulps. Lili-ann and Sture laughed, and I thought it was quite funny, too. After I'd eaten some of everything that was on the table, and taken my finger and scraped the bottom of my oatmeal bowl clean, I was so stuffed, my stomach hurt. But that was good, I thought, because you never knew when you'd get your next meal. I left the table and went to my room and got dressed. I put on a pair of jeans and a T-shirt. Lili-ann wanted me to hop into the shower, but I refused because I was totally clean and it was completely unnecessary. It was weird how people here wasted water. Did people in Sweden really shower at night and then again in the morning? They must have all the water they wanted.

After I got dressed, I went into Lili-ann and Sture's office. There was a globe on the desk. It was blue, and if you pushed the button on it, the globe lit up. I yelled, "Lili-ann," but quickly changed that to

"Mama." It made her sad when I didn't call her Mama, so I'd started calling Lili-ann "Mama" and Sture, "Dad." I wanted to understand how the globe worked. Mama spun the globe a little and showed me South America and Brazil, and I could see Brazil's name on the globe. Then she pointed to Sweden. She pointed to the blue that was the ocean between Brazil and Sweden and said the Swedish word for water first and then "*água.*" My brain went into overdrive. I spun the globe and looked at Brazil, and then I spun the globe again and looked at Sweden. Mama pointed to Sweden and said that was where we were. I looked at Sweden and thought it looked really long. I glanced at Mama. She was taller than I was. Dad was taller than Mama. And the house we lived in was big. I thought about all the houses in the neighborhood. I couldn't figure out how there was room for them all in that little picture of Sweden on the globe. Then I looked at Brazil, and I couldn't understand how all of São Paulo could fit in that little picture of Brazil. That was when I realized that the countries must be enormous, and the water in between them apparently even bigger. It wasn't until then that I really understood that I wasn't even in Brazil anymore but in a completely different country. The realization that I was as far away as I could get from Brazil and from my real mother made me start crying. Mama understood, and she held me until I was done crying.

"*Universo?*" I asked. Mama looked at me, and I repeated it, this time enunciating the word slowly. "*Uuuniveerso?*" Mama walked over to some books and took one of them from the shelf. She started flipping through it until she finally seemed to find what she was looking for. She set the book on Dad's desk and showed me a picture depicting the universe. The picture was beautiful—I had never seen anything like it before, aside from in my dream the previous night. That was the first time I had seen the universe, and I have always wondered how I could dream of something I'd never seen before. Mama and I sat in the office for a long time chatting, well, more like attempting to communicate. It went better than I'd expected, and we were able to understand each other with very few words. Mama pointed to things and told me what they were called, and I repeated the words after her. The Swedish language was so bizarre. The words all seemed reversed, and there was supposed to be an indefinite article—either an *en* or an *ett*—in front of everything. I did not understand this *en/ett* business at all. There didn't seem to be any rhyme or reason to which article went with which word. Even today, I occasionally still say the wrong one.

The doorbell rang, and I ran to open it. There was a woman there with a child. Mama came to the door and welcomed them in. They were the neighbors, Mama's friend Gunilla and her daughter, Lisa, the same girl who owned the princess bed. We went into the kitchen, and Mama served coffee. As Mama and Gunilla chatted at the table, they periodically glanced over at me. Lisa and I sat on the floor, and she gave me a present. I opened it, and it was a blond doll called Barbie. She had a pink dress, pink shoes, and a pink swimsuit. I thanked Lisa, and we sat there and played. I had learned a few Swedish words, but my brain still had a hard time distinguishing between the Portuguese and Swedish words. I might say something half in Swedish and half in Portuguese like, "Lisa, do you want some *água*?" but in my head, I thought the whole thing was in Swedish. Many people came to see us in those first days. They wanted to congratulate Mama and Dad and get a look at their new kids. I often put on music: in Brazil, my Swedish mother Lili-ann had bought me two cassette tapes of my two favorite groups, Xuxa and New Kids on the Block. I always put on Xuxa when any of Mama's friends came over. I danced for them, and I had a few favorite songs, which I would always rewind to. Mama and her girlfriends watched me dance. They applauded when I finished dancing to a song, and then I put on the next song and kept dancing. Eventually, I so bored these poor people with my dancing that Mama was forced to ask me to stop.

I didn't feel insecure where I was now. I wasn't afraid of my new parents. But my security came primarily from within, from my heart. I had brought a small piece of my pride with me, a little part of my world and of myself into this new realm. I had my brother, and I needed to take care of him. I was back to taking things one day at a time and adapting to survive.

I had a responsibility and a promise to keep to the person I loved most.

The Information I'd Waited Twenty-Four Years For

2015

Today is the day I've been looking forward to most of all, which I've longed for, but also dreaded the most. Rivia and I are going to meet the researcher who's been looking for my mother and my family. Today I will find out whether my life is going to change.

We sit in the hotel room, waiting. The researcher, Brian, is originally from the United States but has spent the last twenty years in Brazil. He lives here in São Paulo and is married to a Brazilian. I don't really know what to do with myself, so I open the door to the balcony and step outside. Our room is on one of the uppermost floors, and I feel dizzy when I look down over the railing. I look out over the surrounding buildings. São Paulo is a concrete city, a city of many millions, a city that never sleeps. I step back into the hotel room and close the balcony door behind me to muffle the traffic noise from the streets below. We wait. I try to get a handle on what I'm feeling, but I shut down. I tell myself that whatever happens in the next twenty minutes, we'll deal with it, the two of me, Christina and Christiana. Just like we've dealt with so many other things over the years.

There's a knock on the door, and Rivia's eyes meet mine. Here it comes, the moment I've been waiting twenty-four years for. I walk over to the door and open it. Brian, whom I've never met before, stands before me. He looks happy, friendly, and a little wound up. I tuck that away in the back of my mind as a positive sign. If he were bearing bad news, he wouldn't look so happy, would he? I sit down at the table, and Brian sits across from me. My pulse speeds up, and my sweat glands start producing an unnatural amount of sweat. I start to wonder if he can see my nose sweating, which always happens when I'm nervous. He says that he's located part of my family. My heart beats a little harder; my right hand travels up to my nose and wipes away some small beads of sweat. He's found my mother's sisters and some of my cousins. I smile and hear myself say, "OK, how nice. Have you met them?"

He tells me that he's talked to them, and I ask him if they remember me. I don't have many memories left of my family other than my mother. But I do have a few memories of a woman I always thought was my mother's sister. I remember how my mother and this woman pierced my ears. It hurt, but I was very pleased afterward.

"They remember you, and they're glad that you're back. They're really looking forward to meeting you. They told me a bunch of stories from when you were little," Brian says.

I smile, and even though it's disconcerting to talk to a total stranger about my biological family that I hardly remember, I feel a delightful, warm sensation welling up in me. I ask Brian if the family said I was mischievous and climbed a lot. Brian laughs a little and says that's exactly what they said. It feels good to receive confirmation that I had guessed correctly, and also that these people and I share more than blood, that we also share memories.

Brian tells me that my family lives in Belo Horizonte and that they're eager to meet with me. I'm happy to hear him say that, but now I'm thinking of only one thing: my mother.

"And my mother?" I ask.

I try to read his body language. He looks relaxed. His eyes don't wander when I mention my mother, which they would have done if he hadn't found her or if she were no longer alive. As a little girl, I had learned to read people's body language quickly to gauge their intentions, whether good or bad. My heart beats hard inside my ribs, and I try to demonstrate control through my posture. I glance at Brian. He opens his mouth, and as he does, I focus all my energy on thinking positive thoughts, thinking that the words that will come out of his mouth now will be that my mother is alive. I know that energy and positive thinking won't change the information he brings. And yet that is precisely what every cell in my body is focused on. And then I hear Brian say, "I have found your mother."

I have a thousand questions; yet, my head is completely blank. Something happens to my heart, and the muscles in my face tense. I squeeze my lips together harder, and my eyes well up. I look for con-firmation that I've heard him correctly. "You've found my mother?" I glance over at Rivia, see that she has tears in her eyes, too, and she gives me a little smile, which I return, but I wonder if maybe it looks like I'm making a face. I ask Brian if my mother is doing all right and where she lives.

Brian starts to tell the whole story of how he found my mother, mostly thanks to her name, Petronilia, which is an uncommon name in Brazil. Through the court records, he was able to locate her sisters, and from there he was able to determine that my mother is no longer living on the streets. In terms of her health, she's doing well, but everything is not problem-free.

I wipe away a tear that's rolling down my cheek. He says that my mother also lives in Belo Horizonte and that they're expecting me this weekend. I pick up the phone and call home to Sweden, to my brother. Patrick expects me to call as soon as I have any news. I hear his familiar voice. I tell him that I've just met Brian, that he's told me about our aunts and cousins, and that he has found Mamãe. I hear Patrick repeat,

"He has found Mamãe. Is she alive?" I smile and confirm with a yes. "How's she doing?" he asks. It touches me that he asks. We have completely different relationships with our biological mother. Unlike me, Patrick doesn't have any memories of her. For him, she's the woman who gave birth to him and couldn't take care of him, so I find this conversation particularly heartwarming. We chat for a bit, and I can hear that he's moved. I tell him that he can call if he wants to talk more. I say that I love him and that we'll see each other when he joins me in Brazil in a few days.

This is the day when I, after so many years of not knowing, have learned that my mother is still alive, that she misses me, and that we'll get to see each other soon. This is the day I've found out that I have a family here in Brazil and that they seem to be looking forward to seeing me. This is the day that makes twenty-four years feel both like an eternity and a few seconds. There's nothing more I can say about this day.

Everyday Life in Vindeln
1990s

A lot of things were different in Sweden. My Swedish parents warned me about going over to a stranger's house or talking to strangers. In Brazil, my mother warned me about the police. Some of the policemen were not to be trusted. The trouble was knowing which ones you could trust and which ones you should run away from. So, I did the most logical thing: I ran away from all policemen.

I ran the first time I saw a policeman in Vindeln. Vindeln had its own little police station—more like an office with one policeman who worked there full-time. He lived on the same block as I did. It turned out he was a nice man, but of course I didn't know that at the time. Lisa—who lived next door and was now one of my new Swedish friends—and I were taking a walk through the village. It was summer, and I'd been living in Vindeln for about a month. We'd bought ice-cream cones and had just walked by the movie theater, which was about three hundred feet from the police station. Out stepped the policeman. I saw him and froze. I looked at Lisa, and she looked at me. The policeman turned and saw us. I looked at Lisa again, flung my ice cream on the ground, grabbed her hand, and yelled, "Run!"

Lisa did not resist, but she looked surprised, and she was not moving very fast. I looked back over my shoulder and noticed that the policeman didn't seem to be following us. What I saw instead was a mildly irritated Lisa with ice cream smeared across half her face. After we rounded the corner, I stopped to make sure we were not being followed. Lisa wondered what the heck I was doing, and in my broken Swedish, I asked her why she didn't run. I practically had to drag her for half the distance. Lisa wondered why she *should* run. It occurred to me that maybe I'd done something wrong, because Lisa was giving me the weirdest look.

"Don't children in Sweden learn to run from the police?" I asked. Lisa looked at me as if I were stupid.

"Why would we run from them?" she asked, surprised.

"Because the police beat people," I replied.

"They do not! They're nice."

"Nice?" I wondered aloud, skeptical.

"Yes, nice. Aren't they nice where you come from?"

I didn't know what to say, since I didn't want to admit the truth. I instinctively realized it would sound rude, so I gave a response I'd learned from observing other Swedish children: "I don't know . . ." And I shrugged slightly.

Lisa and I started walking home again. At my insistence, we skirted the police station, even though that made the walk home a little longer. Lisa let me taste her ice cream. I asked her why she wasn't that fast. I'd never seen anyone run so slowly before, and Lisa just told me she didn't like to run. I didn't understand how a person couldn't like to run, but I was glad she shared her ice cream with me.

In the early 1990s, about twenty-five hundred people lived in Vindeln, compared to the sixteen to seventeen million who lived in São Paulo. In Vindeln, you didn't lock your front door if you went out, and if you did, you left your key in the mailbox, which frustrated me. It made no sense to lock the door if you were just going to leave the key ten feet away, where everyone could find it. In São Paulo, there were high walls around the expensive buildings and sometimes dogs and guards. Of course, I preferred and continue to prefer the trust that exists in Swedish society. But I experienced a lot of culture shock as an eight-year-old in Sweden. Whether it had to do with food, religion, clothing, snow, school, friendship, or how the society was set up, yes, everything was different. When everything is new, it's both frightening and exciting. Now I'm grateful for what all the culture shock did for me as a child, and what it still does for me as an adult. But it wasn't always easy when I was little. I discovered that the longer I lived in Vindeln, the easier it became for me to understand how my new family and my new friends thought.

I discovered the way I used to think was starting to change. I started to adjust, and it happened intuitively and at lightning speed. Did what I'd learned in Brazil apply to the situation I was in now in Sweden? What would my new Swedish buddies do in the situation I was in now? What would my Brazilian friends do? The next time I saw that same policeman, I turned to Sara, the pal I was with at the time, and asked her if we should run. Sara told me we shouldn't run from the police, a piece of advice I followed after that, even though I always remained a little on my guard. Certain types of fear penetrate deep into the soul, and even to this day, a small part of me wants to run when I see the police.

In my new family, I noticed that many times tough questions would be glossed over. I couldn't really understand why grown-ups chose to do what I interpreted as lying to their children. When it came to questions about where babies come from, for example, there were eight-year-olds who in all seriousness believed that storks flew to people's homes to deliver a baby to its parents. That was very confusing to me, and I cleared things up for the kids by explaining to them how babies were made. Not all the parents appreciated this.

But even in my first week there, I met several children who would become my friends. Malin, who lived next door; Lisa, the girl who had "my" bed; and Nina, Sara, and Anna, whose mother, Maj, was a daycare worker. I remember one sunny morning when Mama, Patrick, and I were standing on the lawn next to our garage and Maj came over. Patrick was playing in the grass. He wasn't even two yet. While Maj and Mama chatted, Patrick got hold of the hose that Mama had turned on to water the bushes by the corner of the fence. I caught the mischievous gleam in his eye, and then he took the hose and sprayed Maj with the water. She yelped, and Mama also got drenched, trying to get the hose away from him. The whole scene was so hilarious to me as I stood looking on, and I laughed and laughed, and I remember yelling and cheering him on. Patrick was very pleased with himself. Mama was laughing, too, and took off her glasses to dry them on her shirt.

As I mentioned earlier, my first real friend in Sweden was named Maja. She stopped by one day when I was standing outside our house by the mailbox, holding Patrick in my arms. Maja was carrying a black cat that she let me pet. I asked the cat's name, and Maja said it was named Kurre. Maja was nice and blond, and she was a bit like Patricia. I also got to know the parents of some of my playmates and one of my mama's friends that she spent a lot of time with, Ann-Marie, and her husband, Kjell-Arne, who would be there for me later in my life when I needed them.

I remember trying to think about what Mamãe looked like. But after just a couple of months in Sweden, I noticed that I was having a hard time picturing her. I panicked. I couldn't picture my real mother. I knew what she looked like, but I couldn't visualize her. What was going on? I knew that she had short, black hair, that she had brown eyes, and that her lips looked like mine. I remembered how tall she was and what her body looked like. I remembered all the details, but I couldn't picture her. I had trouble breathing. There was a tightness in my chest. I wanted to scream, but I couldn't breathe. Should I yell for my new parents? But then they would see me completely distraught and think I wasn't happy in their lovely home. I tried to calm myself down. I thought to myself, *Breathe, Christiana, breathe. You've been through worse. No need to worry. Everything's going to be OK again. Think about Patrique! You deserve to suffer a little, you know.*

As an adult, when I look back on this incident, I understand that I was suffering a panic attack. It was intense, because it lasted awhile, and I was in extraordinary pain, both physically and mentally. I've often wondered why I didn't call out to my new parents. After all, they had been very nice. I think it was a combination of factors. I didn't want to disappoint them. They had given me and my brother so much, and it would be very unappreciative of me. Also, if I let them help me, it would mean that I'd let them into my life, and I was not ready to do that. But most of all, I think that my pride wouldn't allow me to do it. I was tough, and I could handle things on my own. I was too proud to ask for help, a weakness that has followed me for a large part of my life.

So, I calmed myself down and pushed aside my anxiety. I couldn't accept that my memories of the people I loved would fade away. I couldn't accept that my memories from Brazil, good and bad, would fade away. If I let it happen, I would lose myself. I would lose who I was and wander eternally in darkness. I would fail Mamãe, Camile, Patricia, the boy I'd killed—and I would fail myself and my brother. It was my job to tell him the truth, tell him how wonderful and loving our mother was. I couldn't forget. Camile had told me that as long as we held each other in our hearts, as long as we remembered each other, we would always be together. I needed to hold on to her, and to Mamãe, and all my memories. I decided that if I thought about them the whole time, they would always be there for me. I lay down on my back, stared up at the ceiling, and started replaying all the memories I had from my time in the forest, things that had happened on the streets, Camile and her stories, Mamãe and her sacrifices, her suffering, and her love. I thought about the boy I'd killed, and I cried. I ran through everything I could remember from the orphanage, and I remembered my last moment with Mamãe. I still held all the memories of my life in Brazil up until the moment I, my brother, and our new parents stepped into our big red house in Vindeln. If I did this every night before I fell asleep, I would never forget the people I loved, and I would never forget who I was.

What I didn't know then was that when you try to hold on to the past as hard as I was, you sometimes miss out on living in the present. I wish that someone had told me, *Christina, live in the moment and dream of the future.* That doesn't mean you lose yourself. But stopping where you are now will cost you more than you can imagine.

I remember my first summer in Sweden being fun, full of playing with my new friends, but I felt different. First of all, none of them looked like me. A few of the kids had told their parents that I was brown—not in a mean way but more out of curiosity. Some of the parents were a little uncomfortable and unsure how to explain to their children why I was chocolatey brown. They often replied that I came from a country where it was super warm and the sun was always shining, which is why I was brown.

I thought that explanation was kind of weird, since there were plenty of white people in Brazil. Plus, I was astounded by how naïve the children in Sweden were. They seemed to think that all adults were nice and that you should always do what they said. The only thing I heard that deviated from this belief that all adults were nice was people saying you shouldn't go off with strangers. Hello? Surely everyone knew that!

The children here didn't seem to have any concerns besides falling off their bikes and scraping their knees, not getting the exact doll they had wished for, not being allowed to watch unlimited amounts of TV, having to go outside and play, or not wanting to go to bed at a certain time. It was very confusing to me and hard to fathom.

Naturally, all the things I'd experienced seemed completely unreal to them. Whenever I mentioned something that had happened to me, I always regretted it. They really couldn't relate to my experiences, and their emotional lives just weren't the same. When I did share things, they thought I was making them up or that they had come out of some wicked fairy tale. So, I started making things up. I might as well turn it into a good fairy tale. For example, I made up a story about how I had wrestled a lion and that I knew karate, which I absolutely did not. I could have easily taken them all in a fight, so I might as well say that I could. I made up all kinds of things. I lied to my parents as well. Whenever they wondered something and asked about Mamãe, I didn't want to hurt their feelings by telling them that I loved Mamãe and not them. So, I told them what I thought they wanted to hear. I minimized my birth mother, pretended I thought she was dumb and that I was happy to be in Sweden. I wanted to fit in, even though I really didn't. I wanted to be nice to my parents, because I understood that they genuinely cared about me, but on the inside a part of me wanted to scream. And I argued with my new parents a lot. I would yell at them that they couldn't tell me what to do, that they weren't my real parents, and that I could do what I wanted.

At times like these, a part of me came back to life and tried to cry for help, tried to get someone to see how unbelievably sad and broken I was. But no one saw or knew what to do about it. So, Dad would grab me by the ear and lead me to my room and tell me I couldn't come out until I'd calmed down. I had to learn all on my own to suppress the flames and try to become someone who wasn't me, someone who could fit in, someone like the person my parents, my new friends, and their families expected me to be.

Then it was August, and the start of school approached. I'd learned Swedish in just two months. However, I did have an accent, and I'd forgotten almost all of my Portuguese, or as I called it then, Brazilian. I had to start in first grade, one grade below my friends who were the same age as I was. But it took the teachers only a few weeks to realize that I knew enough to switch to second grade. I did everything I could in those first few weeks to show that I was a super good student. I realized there was a chance the kids would tease me for being older than they were. And I didn't need anything else that might cause me to be bullied or excluded.

I remember the first time I was introduced to my future class. The teacher's name was Barbro. She was calm and gentle. She told my future classmates that they would be welcoming a new girl to their class that day. Her name was Christina Rickardsson and she was from Brazil, and the children should be nice and considerate. I remember the feeling before I opened that door to face my new classmates. *Make a good impression. Don't let them see that you're nervous or scared—they'll eat you alive. Smile, look happy.* I opened the door and stepped decisively into the frightening room, wearing the biggest smile I could muster, my back straight. My heart was pounding extra hard, and I said hello to all the kids in the best Swedish I could manage.

All the kids looked at me, some stared, others smiled, everyone looked curious. Suddenly, one of the boys opened his mouth and told the teacher and the rest of the class, "But, teacher, that's not a girl. That's a boy."

I remember how my eyes hardened and how I stared at that boy, Christopher, and I understood that he was the one who was going to make things hard for me. I knew my short, Afrolike hair was different from that of the other girls in Vindeln. They all had long, straight hair. And thus began a new period of my life. I got into a lot of fights.

One thing I learned quickly was that Swedish children were not as good at fighting as I was. The girls basically had no idea how to fight. And the boys had not had the same training as I had. Then came the attempts at bullying. That same kid who'd called me a boy also called me the N-word on the playground at recess in front of all the other kids. I punched him, and then I informed him that I was not black, I was Latina, and that if he wanted to call me anything, he ought to stick to the facts.

I was summoned to the principal's office because I'd punched that kid and knocked the wind out of him. My dad had to come to the school. We sat there in the principal's office, and my dad listened to what had happened and how I'd behaved. *Girls don't behave that way.* My father, who very clearly did not like that other children were calling me the N-word, told the principal that his daughter was right to defend herself and that it was a good thing I knew how to do that.

I was involved in a lot of fights and quite a few dustups in the beginning, but I stood up for myself. I fought, and I was not bullied. I had hung out with tougher kids and run in tougher circles. More than anything, I wanted to be accepted, to be one of the gang, to have friends and fit in.

Maybe that sounds simple, but it wasn't. Every time someone used a racial slur, it hurt. It was the intention behind the word that hurt. What they were saying was that I wasn't one of them, not worth as much. And that no matter how hard I tried, I would never be one of them, because I was always going to have brown skin and black eyes and nappy hair.

I never showed the children my pain. I never cried in front of them, and I fought back until they understood that I was not going to be bullied. I decided that the life I'd had in Brazil was not going to follow me here. In Brazil, people used to spit on me and say I wasn't worth as much as they were. These early months in Sweden were a time when I questioned many things and when I had to find answers and solutions on my own. The teachers at the school were fine, but no one knew what was going on inside me. I was split in two, and even though I had a lot of wonderful girlfriends, I wasn't big on playing doctor or pretending little plastic horses were real. I wanted to climb, build little huts, do sports. At recess, the boys played sports in the school yard, and I wanted to play with them. I understood the importance of having female friends, but I was happier with the boys. Not just because sports were more fun and easier for me to understand, but also because the social code was different with the boys. Their behavior was so different from the girls'. They said what they thought and what they liked, and that made it easier for me. If a problem came up, we fought and then it was resolved. With the girls, I could be playing and then suddenly realize that they were all exchanging these weird looks. Then I would know that I'd said or done something that wasn't right, but no one would tell me exactly what I'd done. I remember wondering how in the world I was going to learn right from wrong if they wouldn't tell me what I'd done wrong. I understood that there were a bunch of unwritten rules that I needed to learn. If I mastered those, I would fit in better. So, I made sure to learn the social norms. I changed who I was, and over time I gradually fit in with my peers. I became one of them. They came to see me as Swedish. They might have stopped seeing me as Brazilian, but I hadn't.

I remember the first time I saw snow. It had been a dark, rainy fall, and I had noticed that the darkness made me more tired. One night it snowed. That morning, I woke up as usual and walked into the kitchen where Mama had made oatmeal and hardboiled eggs. That was what I ate every morning. I looked out the big kitchen window and to my astonishment it wasn't dark and rainy. It was white. Everything was white. It was as if we were in a cloud. A beautiful, thick, untouched blanket of white powder covered the grass, the trees, and the street. I was completely beside myself and raced outside, wearing only my underwear. From somewhere, I heard Mama yelling my name, but I didn't care. I threw open the front door and rolled in the snow on the lawn.

It took my brain a few seconds to realize that the beautiful whiteness called snow was as cold as the dickens—bitingly cold, painfully cold. Ow, ow, ow! I popped back up and ran screaming up the stairs toward the front door where Mama was waiting, trying hard not to laugh. She tossed me into the shower and sprayed warm water on me. After my body finally warmed up and after she literally pried the showerhead out of my hands, she insisted that I get dressed and go to school. I told her I was not going back out into the cold, but Mama said that all children do. I responded that all children most assuredly did not. The children in Brazil sure didn't. Mama smiled and said that we were in Sweden and Swedish children definitely did. After I put on snow pants and a coat, my classmates and my friend Sara and I all walked to school.

When the bell rang for the first recess, all the children were up in a flash and out in the snow. By the time I got out onto the school yard, I saw that the children were playing in the snow and ruining it. It made me feel anxious to see them building snowmen and snow lanterns and running around and ruining the beautiful snow. My anxiety turned to panic when I realized that if I didn't save any of the beautiful snow, the children would wreck it all. I feverishly scanned the playground and spotted an area to my right where the children hadn't had a chance to ruin the snow yet. I ran over and drew a big circle in the snow and positioned myself right in front of the ring, and then I yelled to the other kids that that snow was mine. What I did not understand was that I had apparently yelled, "Drop what you're doing and come take my snow!" Because that was exactly what the children did. They saw it as a game, but to me it was dead serious. They all started running over to take my snow. I got so mad, I was practically sobbing. The children were running around, trying to take my snow, and I watched the beautiful snow that I was trying to protect being ruined. I, former street child that I was, reacted the only way I knew how or could. I ran around hitting the children who took my snow while at the same time screaming, "My snow! It's my snow!" It didn't matter whether the children were the same age as I was or whether they were three years older. They all took a licking.

I was summoned to the principal's office. Principal Gunnar explained that the snow belonged to everyone. I sat directly across from him with my arms crossed, thinking, *How dumb can you be? Nothing belongs to everyone.*

One Day in the Favela

2015

Brasilândia is one of the world's biggest favelas and São Paulo's largest slum, where about 4.2 million people live. Today, Rivia and I are going there. I wake up with mixed emotions on this sunny but not especially warm morning in São Paulo. It feels exciting, and I know that it's the adventurous, Swedish side of me that feels this way. Slums are a completely different world, a world you see only on TV and in the movies.

Then the other side of me rears its head. I remember my own life there. I see that little girl running and playing in the mud with what she has found in the trash. I picture Camile, Santos, and myself making kites out of bamboo, old plastic bags, and string. I remember the joy and love I felt for both of them. I smile as I see us running as hard as we can, trailing the kite behind us. I hear us laughing. We're barefoot as we run, and it's hot. I remember how we swim together and how we take care of one another when one of us gets sick. But I also see the lonely, hungry, sad girl, the girl who's running, not only when she's playing but also when she needs to escape, the girl who is also me. Suddenly I see a completely different world than the one on TV and in the movies, a world that is a part of my history, a part of me.

It is not safe to enter these neighborhoods without a guide, and since I don't speak the language anymore, it doesn't feel like an option at all. Brian, who has helped us with so much down here, has contacts in Brasilândia, and he has requested permission for us to enter.

When we get into the car to drive there, Brian tells us about a housing project in the favela he's worked on. The project is to help people who live in the area. They're replacing the little sheet-metal, wood, and cardboard shacks with tiny brick homes. There are people who want to help, there are things being done, but it's far from what's needed.

The sun is broiling as we drive, and Brian tells us about the situation in Brazil, about the different neighborhoods we pass and about the corruption in the country, what the various presidents have done and not done. We drive past a large soccer stadium with lots of buses parked outside—so many buses but no people. The place is deserted. Brazil invested billions in building big, beautiful soccer stadiums all over the country for the World Cup. Now they're empty and unused while people live in extreme poverty. Many of the stadiums have become parking lots. Imagine if the money had been used for the needy instead.

Brazil, the fifth largest country in the world with a population of more than two hundred million, has a tremendous wealth of natural resources, but the nation has not succeeded in reducing the enormous gap between the rich and the poor. The numbers are frightening: 60 to 70 percent of the total assets go to the wealthiest 10 percent, and scarcely 2 percent go to the poorest 20 percent.

Brian, who likes to talk, tells us funny but tragic stories about how politicians in Brazil line their own pockets. He says it's become part of Brazilian culture. We read about it in the papers every day. The rich in São Paulo take helicopters from meeting to meeting to avoid the traffic and avoid being robbed in their cars. Everyone knows about the situation, but it seems impossible to do anything about it.

The car ride passes quickly, and we are approaching the favela now. The city with its skyscrapers is visible in the distance behind us, and now mountains of tiny houses and shanties built on top of one another tower in front of us. We stop the car at the outskirts of the favela and get out. A wide brook runs to the left of the car. I recognize its scent, or rather its stench, immediately. I walk around the car and see that the brook is filled with junk and trash.

We're met by a stout, dark-skinned woman, Tatiane J. Silva, who beams at us with a big smile. We hug and exchange greetings, and once again I'm frustrated that I don't speak the language. If they would at least stop talking both when they inhale and when they exhale, I might have a chance of catching a few words. But they talk fast and generally toss in some arm waving and raise their pitch, which I myself have never done. During this trip, I have laughed to see Rivia flip from a calm Swedish pace to speaking Portuguese, where her tone changes and she gesticulates more and more. Incredibly charming, I think, but obviously it would be more fun if I could understand what she is saying.

The woman invites us into her little house, which consists of two small rooms. Everything is crammed in. There are two small hot plates, and in the back room there is a very basic toilet. I see that she has a flat-screen TV, and I smile. Memories from when I was little and running around in similar neighborhoods with my street buddies come back to me. How we used to gather around someone's little cathode-ray TV, which was showing mostly static, to watch a soccer game. We could hardly see anything, and we pretty much followed what was going on in the game based on the reactions of the people sitting closest to the TV.

We step out of the tiny house and start walking toward the favela. We stop at a kiosk, and I buy a *dimdim*, an ice cream that I loved when I was little and which Camile and I used to buy when we had the money. This time they have my favorite flavor, coconut, and I buy one for me and one for Rivia. I bite the plastic wrapper open and immediately start sucking up the ice cream. The feeling of being six and seven years old again sneaks over me, and I recognize the taste, which brings back memories of mischievous games and laughter. A man named Leonardo meets us. He says that he'll be our guide for the day. Brian has had to ask the people "in charge" of the area—the gangs and drug dealers who call the shots here—for permission to bring us in.

We start our walking tour up the mountain between shacks and brick houses. Here and there, water smelling of sewage flows by. The red dirt, the classic Brazilian red dirt, is redder than I remember it. We walk past plants that I recognize, and one of them has a bunch of little green balls that look like burrs. A lost memory comes flooding back. I picture us kids running around and throwing the little green burr balls at one another, trying to get them to stick in one another's hair. Whoever has the most burrs in their hair loses. I break off a part of the plant and take it with me on our tour.

We meet various people, and I start to notice that some of them are keeping an eye on us. I ask Brian about it, and he says they're watching us to make sure we don't take pictures or film anything that's not OK. We wander farther and make a few stops along the way so I can "play monkey," climbing up onto various things to take pictures of the area but also pictures of myself, my arms outstretched like the statue of Christ in Rio de Janeiro. Everything is surreal, and a remarkable joy bubbles up in me as I wander up to the top. Leonardo, who lives in the favela with his family, tells us what life is like and how things work in Brasilândia.

On the way to the top, we run into a gang of kids who start following us. A little girl sees what I'm holding, and she picks her own little green balls and starts throwing them at me, laughing. The child in me wakes up immediately, and I respond by throwing balls at her, but none of them stick in her hair. We run around and chase each other and throw balls at each other. I'm not in good enough shape to keep going and after a while simply have to concede that not only is this little girl able to run farther than I am, but she's also much better at the game. Rivia helps me pick the burrs out of my hair.

The boys who were following us from a bit of a distance come closer to us now and start chatting. I try to say a few words to them, but, in the end, Rivia does the talking. They follow us for a long time, and we stop once in a while because they want to tell us something or show us something. When we start approaching the top, one of the boys, who's named Jonas, gives me his baseball hat and his eyeglasses. I don't really understand why, but I can tell he wants me to put them on. I put on his leopard-print cap and sunglasses, which are way too small, and then he points to my iPhone and says, "Selfie." I burst out laughing. Of course the kids in the favela know the word *selfie*. We take a selfie together. Jonas and his friend look at the picture, nod, and say it's approved. Then he points to my iPhone 4S and says that his brother has a newer and better iPhone. I smile, am about to ask him how his brother got it, but I'm quite sure that I already know the answer to that question. So, I just say mine's good enough and tousle his curly hair a little. He pulls back, laughing. They follow us for our whole tour through the slum. They're happy and mischievous and have so much energy.

When we reach the top of the favela, there is a little bar—or more accurately a little shack with a white sign with the word "Bar" painted on it in red. A man wearing a Brazilian national team jersey is drinking a beer. He seems to be the owner of the bar. He wants to sell us a beer, but we politely decline. We're not allowed to leave, though, until he gets a hug from Rivia and me. Before we start our trek back down, we stop to photograph the patchwork quilt of little shacks and brick houses that lies before us and extends as far as the eye can see. The thought of 4.2 million people here in one of the world's biggest slums is completely unfathomable. You'll find joy and pain here—so many memories for me, so many emotions. We head back to the car, walking between narrow alleys, and I see myself as a young girl running down these alleys, sometimes fleeing, sometimes playing. I look around and take in what I see, the vast patchwork, and far away in the distance, the high-rises of São Paulo, two different worlds in the very same city. Electrical wires that have been strung from shack to shack, completely unprotected; small cars in a variety of colors here and there. One life here and one life in Sweden. They are so different, I think. And yet it feels like joy and happiness are appreciated more here. Shouldn't it be the other way around? Shouldn't we be grateful and happy in Sweden about how well we're doing? Or are we like the corrupt Brazilian politicians who only want more and more and forget or lose the ability to appreciate what we have?

Our guide wants us to meet his family before we conclude the day. Once we reach his "house," we meet his wife. She's my age and has four children. They live with her parents. I try to follow the conversation as I tally up the nine people who live in this tiny home. There's a ton of other children here now, too, and, in the end, I give up on counting and decide there are way too many people living in this little shack. They are incredibly nice and hospitable. They get out the best they have at home to offer, which is popcorn and Coca-Cola. After spending the whole day walking around the favela and touching everything from plants to dirt, I really have no desire to stuff my hand into the popcorn bowl and then bring these bacteria into my mouth. A voice in the back of my head thoroughly chastises me. Here I stand with these fantastic people who are sharing what little they have with me, and I'm thinking about bacteria. I dispatch my right hand into the bowl and scoop up some popcorn, thank them in Portuguese, and eat. I throw in a little prayer to the powers that be that I won't get a stomach virus or food poisoning or anything else, and hope that those eight years when I ate every conceivable filthy thing I could find have made my stomach immune.

We have a wonderful time, and even though the elderly man in the house is drunk, despite it being the middle of the day, he also seems happy and content. He hugs me, and I smile and hug him back. He holds me for a little too long, and I suddenly no longer feel comfortable with the situation. I force myself to smile and try to get out of his grasp. I'm about to succeed, when his wife joins the hug and it feels a little better. She starts chatting with me, and everyone has more or less gathered around me now. They're all curious about my history. I hear Rivia start to tell my story for what feels like the hundredth time. They ask a bunch of questions, and I try to answer them all. It's strange how you can be away from a place for so long and yet so much can still feel familiar when you return. An elderly woman says that she's proud of me, and I'm a little surprised. What have I done for this woman who's barely even known me for an hour to feel proud of me? Rivia tells me that she says, "You're Brazilian, and you haven't forgotten your roots, and now you're here to see us. You haven't forgotten us, your people." I admit that she's right. This is a part of me, and I haven't forgotten or tried to deny this part of my life. I've just been in a different part of the world.

These people have a lot of love and warmth. They have so little, but what little they have, they offer to share, and they do so with happiness and pride. I feel proud to have my roots here, despite all the injustices, despite all the horrors, in this warmhearted country, among these warmhearted people. We thank our hosts and walk the last little way down to our car.

What a day! At the car, we all stand around chatting for a bit, and a boy comes running by with his homemade kite. I ask Rivia to ask him if I can try it. He's a little skeptical at first, but eventually he hands me the string attached to his already airborne kite. I take it and run a little. It's a wonderful sensation to let the child in me play a little . . . *Oh, no, no* . . . There are electrical wires everywhere, and the kite gets stuck. The boy looks less happy when I hand back the kite string with the kite now tangled in the wires. I smile apologetically and pull some candy out of my bag to give him. The boy looks happy again, and I have the sense that he'll get the kite down by himself. I have no choice but to admit that the intervening years have definitely turned me into a lousy kite flyer.

I leave the favela completely exhausted but feeling wonderful inside. It's not where you come from; it's where you belong that matters. And it's OK to feel like you belong in more than one place.

With Mama in the City of Angels
1990s

One day when I was twelve, Mama and Dad yelled for me. They were in the bedroom. There was something in Dad's voice that didn't sound right. What had I done now?

Mama was half lying, half sitting in bed on the pink quilt she'd made. Dad was sitting on the edge of the bed next to Mama, holding her hand. They asked me to come in and then come closer. Mama looked sad, but tough at the same time. I'd always thought of Mama as weak. She was frail, the opposite of me. She was so gentle and always understanding. Dad was more decisive, hard, and if I was anyone's girl, I was mostly Dad's. He let me work and help out, and he viewed me as strong. Mama always wanted me to be a girl, a child. How was I supposed to explain to her that I wasn't like her, that the soft part of me had withered away and there wasn't much of it left? We were as different as people can be.

"Christina, come sit here next to us," Mama said.

This didn't feel right. This felt very wrong. A sickening sensation spread through me, a feeling I'd had so many times in Brazil. *Run!* my senses screamed. *Get out of this room now!*

I could hear my parents' voices talking to me, but I didn't really know what they were saying. I just felt so weird. Then I heard Mama say the word *sick*, and I snapped out of it. Had she said cancer? Liver cancer? I didn't know that much about diseases, but I knew that cancer killed people. Mama and Dad chatted about how the disease could be treated and so on. But I knew better. I knew that this was death again. It didn't matter where I was in the world, death would always find me. The worst part of it was that death didn't take me. It took everyone else around me, everyone who cared about me.

I don't remember what I said to them. I remember only how I ran down the stairs to the basement where my room was. I don't remember if I shut the door or slammed it. I flung myself on my bed and cried. I was so angry. There are no words for how heartbroken I was. Alone in my room, I said out loud to God, the angels, and to myself, *It isn't fair, because she's good! Take me instead! Please, please take me! I don't want everyone I love to be taken away.* That was when I knew that I loved Mama. I had worked so hard at not loving her, not letting her in. So many times I had yelled at her that she wasn't my real mother and that she couldn't tell me what to do, but somehow her love had always made it through. I was so angry. Why was I being forced to care about her? It made it so much harder to lose her. Everyone I loved had been taken away or died or left me alone in a world I didn't understand and that didn't understand me.

God, whatever I've done, please, tell me, show me so that I can make it right again! It's not fair to hurt other people because of what I've done. But I knew that God wasn't listening, and, on some level, I understood that that wasn't how the universe worked. I could hear a nasty voice in the back of my head. It was my voice, and it whispered, *You know what you did, and you know why you're being punished. Did you really believe you could take a life without being punished?*

I knew it was true. I was so sad, but I knew I couldn't change it. I knew that I would always be punished for it. Punishing myself wasn't enough.

I felt so much rage growing up that it frightened me. It filled me and destroyed me. I felt it, but I didn't know how to handle it, so I smiled and laughed even more and did well in school. I had learned to manipulate other people, to make them see someone other than me. They saw a happy little girl who was having a much, much better life and who was grateful for it.

My life had taught me that. I had started doing this on the streets, I became even better at it in the orphanage, and I let it go into full bloom in Sweden. I had walled off my true self. I felt I needed to fit in and stay unnoticed. And people were so easy to manipulate. I knew how far a smile could get you, and I knew the power of a nice word. I had also started to learn how to use words as weapons. But I was also manipulating myself. I wasn't hurting anyone but myself. I wanted to fit in and be like all the other children. But I was different. How could I not be? They played with plastic horses in plastic stables. They knew nothing about life. They had received all kinds of love, but they didn't understand what it was worth. They didn't understand how evil people could be. They knew nothing about death. They didn't know what it was like to lose the only person who had loved you. They didn't know what it was like to live with strangers. They didn't know what it was like to begin to let other people in again, to feel tired, alone, scared, and to pray to God for strength every night even though you knew he had forsaken you.

Sometimes you meet people you only get to be with for a short time. What's difficult is accepting that and moving on. But sometimes that may be what you have to do. Accept that a relationship is only a loan, and when it's not there anymore, you should rejoice at having had the honor of having it at all, of receiving so much without needing to give. Maybe it didn't end the way you wanted or expected. Maybe it ended before it really had a chance to begin, or ended without your having a chance to say goodbye.

The first and only movie that Mama and I watched together in a movie theater was *City of Angels*. It was 1998, and Mama was very sick. I asked her to see it with me, even though Dad didn't think it was such a good idea. We needed to drive from Vindeln to Umeå, a trip that took about fifty minutes, but Mama understood that I wanted to do a mother-daughter thing, that I wanted to have something that was just ours to take with me into my life and remember.

We reserved the tickets and drove to Umeå. The movie was showing in the biggest theater, and we sat right in the middle, a little toward the back. It was about a male angel who falls in love with a human being. She's a doctor, and she falls in love with him, too. Then the angel gives up his immortality for her. They manage to spend one night together, and then she dies in a traffic accident. A beautiful and melancholy film that came to mean so much to Mama and me. It contained everything we never talked about: angels, love, life, but most of all, death.

I remember the tears streaming down my cheeks now and then during the movie, and I tried to wipe them away discreetly without Mama noticing. She cried, too. We saw each other crying but didn't say anything. I'm grateful for those one hundred fourteen minutes that we shared in front of the screen at the movie theater in Umeå. We had never communicated so clearly with each other. Emotions are so powerful. They can say more than words ever can. One glance between us conveyed so much love and pain, fear and hope, and through all this, I think we both knew that we didn't have much time left. We watched and felt; it was as if we were alone in a theater full of people. I wanted to take her hand, but I didn't. At that moment, it would have been like saying goodbye, and we weren't there yet. She lived significantly longer than the doctors had predicted, I think because of us kids. Maybe mostly because of Patrick. Those two had a strong bond. Anyone who claims that blood is thicker than water, that the ties in a family who share the same genes are stronger, does not understand how love works. Mama stuck it out as long as she could. She prolonged her life because she was afraid her family would collapse if she left us too soon.

We have scarcely been able to stick together since she left us. It was an enormous loss. Every day she is with me in my thoughts, and I almost always wear something that belongs to her: a piece of jewelry, clothing, a belt. Something to keep her with me. Even though she fought hard not to leave us, it still came way too soon. She was only fifty, and she deserved so much more. I'm glad that she was able to have the experience of seeing how wonderful her love was for Patrick, and seeing that her love had also reached me. I'm glad that I opened myself to her love, and I know that before she died, she knew that she had my love completely. We—Patrick, Dad, and I—were never the same without her. Our destinies changed, and the pain of losing her broke our hearts and caused us immense grief.

Only now as an adult do I understand what a mother can mean to a family and what Mama's love meant to me. At one time, I saw her as weak, but now I see how strong she was. In solitude she cried about her illness and her awareness that her death was approaching and that she was going to leave us. To the rest of the family and the world, she kept on as if nothing had changed, as if life were as it should be. Not even when she lost all her hair, when she stood in front of the bathroom mirror and watched her femininity being wiped away, even then she didn't break down. I witnessed only one lone tear fall on her cheek as I passed the bathroom on my way to the kitchen. She quickly wiped it away, put on her wig, and walked into the kitchen. She was an amazing woman and an example to me every day. I learned from her that being gentle and nice isn't a weakness but a strength. She fought her illness for four years. Even though the doctors had given her one year to live, at most, she battled on for four years. Witnessing her fight against cancer, but also her struggle to live and stay with us kids, allowed me to really see how strong she was. Being by her side during her chemo treatments made me realize just what vitality she possessed. Despite the all-consuming, debilitating therapy, she still talked about the future and everything she hoped for. We never know our strength until life tests us. But most of all, we don't know what strength and power another person has until we follow them for a while on their journey.

It's not easy saying goodbye, and for Mama and me, it was almost impossible. How do you tell someone that you hope you'll see them again, that you'll see each other on the other side? Is there another side? How can you show your love in the proximity of death, when every emotion you show is like a goodbye? Every day the compact, heavy, painful lump of unspoken emotion grew bigger still in my chest. I was lost, but we didn't talk about it. No one in the family talked about the unavoidable. We took it one day at a time. We felt and we grieved, but we didn't talk.

I knew that the time was coming, but I didn't want to accept it. I wanted to pretend there was time. I wanted to pretend that you would sew me a pink ball gown, like we decided when I was ten, to wear to the prom. I wanted us to go to London, like we'd talked about doing when I got older. I wanted to still have you so you could tell me what I should do when things felt dark and gloomy, when a boy I liked broke my heart, when school felt hard, when I needed love.

How do you say goodbye to the future we pictured, to the future we planned? How do you say goodbye without hurting the other person? Saying goodbye is like saying, You're alive now, but you'll be gone soon, and there's no hope left. How was I supposed to say goodbye when I didn't want to strip you of your hope? As long as you were breathing, we could still pretend there was hope.

So I sat on the edge of my mother's bed at Norrland University Hospital. She had her own room. Dad and Patrick had left the room, which gave us a little time to ourselves. The mood was fraught. The words hung in silence like a dark rain cloud. I sat hunched over, looking at anything and everything other than into my mama's eyes, which I knew were resting on my face. I took a deep breath and looked her in the eye. She gave me a sad little smile, and the heavy lump in my chest grew. I took another deep breath and smiled a fake smile. I asked if there was anything she wanted, if I could get her anything. Mama said she was doing fine.

Fine? This was anything but fine, but I kept quiet. She asked how I was, and I answered, "Fine." Mama asked if I liked the gold bracelet she'd given me for my fourteenth birthday. I said I loved it. She said that when I turned eighteen, I would get the matching necklace. The jewelry had belonged to her mother. I think that was Mama's way of saying goodbye, of saying that she would always be there. I stayed sitting there and held her hand. I remember feeling like I wanted to say something to her, explain that I loved her and say goodbye. I started feeling a sense of panic. It wouldn't be long until Dad and Patrick came back. So, I did the thing I'm worst at; I sang to her. I sang the only song I could think of, and I sang it off-key. I tried to hold my tears back and keep my voice steady.

After that, we sat in silence for a few seconds, which felt like an eternity. My eyes lingered on the floor and Mama's on me. She squeezed my hand to urge me to look at her. I had tears in my eyes, but I held them back. Our eyes met, and Mama said, "Christina, take care of Patrick and Dad."

I looked at her and knew what she wanted me to say, what I was supposed to promise. The words hurt. Eight years earlier, my biological mother had shouted through the orphanage gate that no matter what,

I should take care of Patrique. And here I sat, eight years later, and my adoptive mother was asking the same thing of me. I felt trapped. That was a lifelong promise, and I didn't know if I was strong enough to handle it. I didn't know if I could bear it. But how could I be selfish in this moment and say no, or say that I'd do my best but that I couldn't promise anything? So I responded the way you're supposed to in a situation like that. I said what would give her a little hope for those of us she loved and was leaving. "I'll take care of them, Mama. Don't worry. Patrick will be fine."

I said Patrick because I knew she was probably most worried about him. I mean, he was only eight and was about to lose his mother. I was worried for him, for me, for Dad, and for us as a family. At times like this, it becomes so clear who holds a family together. In our family, Mama was the glue that held us together. She was the interpreter in the family, and through her flexibility, she understood us all. Dad and Patrick walked in right then. Dad was chatting, and Mama turned her attention to him, but she gave me one last look that conveyed strength and a smile that confirmed that she knew that I would be there for them, for Patrick. And then the moment was over. We'd said goodbye to each other without saying goodbye, without saying that we loved each other. I walked over to the window while they chatted and looked out. It was a sunny day, and I looked at the sky without seeing it. Behind me lay my dying mother, her skin yellow, her sick liver unable to clean out the toxins anymore. She was so thin.

Death has the ability to hang over you, enough so that you feel alive but wish to be gone. It reminds us at regular intervals that life is not to be taken for granted. Life reminds us that we don't always get what we want. Life reminds us that death is out there.

Together, my biological mother, Petronilia; my adoptive mother, Lili-ann; and Camile gave me enough warmth for me to be able to clench my teeth when times felt the darkest and not stop walking. Sometimes life offers food scraps from trash cans in a filthy alley in São Paulo, and sometimes it offers a five-course dinner at Grill in Stockholm, Sweden's beautiful capital city. Life is fickle.

My biological mother protected my brother and me as well as she could and wholeheartedly—I don't doubt that for a second. My adoptive mother taught me that in pain there can be love. Camile gave me a friendship that went beyond the ordinary. Two normal women and a girl have made all the difference in my life. I think that we often under-estimate the significance we have to others. We don't fully understand what we can accomplish for another person. What you do with the time you have available is what counts. What we remember often isn't what we received, but rather how it felt to receive it. I've received expensive presents and been happy, but nothing has ever beaten or will ever beat the feeling I had when I got that box of Bon O Bon chocolates from my biological mother when I was lost and alone at the orphanage. Nothing can beat the way I felt when my adoptive mother gave me Helen Exley's book *To a Very Special Daughter* or what I felt when we sat in that movie theater together. Love can't be bought, manufactured, or elicited on request. It's a gift that we choose to give and to receive. It's unselfish and maybe it can't move mountains, but it can do something even better: it can save a life.

Mamãe Petronilia

2015

It's remarkable how you can lose something and then get it back. One thing we all have in common is that we don't know what life has in store for us. From the moment we're born, we're part of what I call the lottery of life. I was ripped away from my biological mother when I was eight years old, got an adoptive mother who then died of cancer, and here I stand now, thirty-two years old, about to be reunited with my biological mother. It's hard to describe exactly what I'm feeling. I don't even know. I'm glad that I get to see her again after twenty-four years, but a part of me is scared. What if I don't feel like she's my mother when I see her? So much has happened to me in the years that have elapsed, and obviously for her, too. What if we don't feel anything for each other? What if I lose the image I have of her as my hero? What happens then, to my story of my childhood? What happens to my memories?

Rivia and I stand beside the parked rental car. We're in Belo Horizonte, which is about two and a half hours by plane, inland from São Paulo, and then six hours by car from Diamantina, where I was born. This is where Mamãe lives now with her sister, my aunt Vitoria.

Brian hasn't told me so much aside from that Mamãe is sick and not doing well. I haven't wanted to hear any more, either. I want to draw my own conclusions and hear about Mamãe's illness from the family. And now here I stand, feeling both elated and scared stiff at the same time. We leave the car and start walking down the little paved slope, about one hundred fifty feet from the address where Mamãe lives. I'm holding on to Rivia's hand tightly when, about thirty feet from the apartment building, I see three older women open the gate and step out onto the sidewalk.

It's strange how the brain works. It's strange that a face you haven't seen in twenty-four years and no longer remember is just suddenly there. I look at the three older women, and without a doubt I know which one is my mother. It's also funny how the body can behave. Without my brain having had a chance to send any conscious signals to it, my body has already started walking toward Mamãe. I see her smile, and I recognize that smile from when I was little. I look her in the eye and see love and warmth there. I hear her talking to me and recognize her voice, even if I don't understand what she's saying now. We hug and I feel my eyes well up, but I hold back the tears. It's strange that a person can maintain so much control while at the same time things just happen that are out of one's control. I take a step back and greet the other two women, Mamãe's sisters, Vitoria and Elsa. There's something familiar about Vitoria, and I realize she must have been the one who was there when I got my ears pierced. We hug, and they seem genuinely happy to see me. I hear my name, Christiana, over and over. I'm Christiana here and no one else. It feels weird, but good.

I hug Mamãe again, and Rivia has already started translating. My family welcomes her just as warmly. While Rivia chats with the others, Mamãe and I get a few seconds to ourselves. I look at her. The woman who was so tall when I was little is now shorter than I am. She has short, curly black hair streaked with silver here and there. Her eyes are dark brown, her teeth straight and beautiful, and I realize they're false. She looks like she's generally doing pretty well. She has big ears, well, bigger than my own measly ones, anyway. We look a lot alike, and I see the similarities between her and Patrick, my brother, even more. Mamãe and I have the same nose, and without my thinking about it, my right hand has traveled up to the right side of my upper lip, and I poke and dab at it with my index finger a few times. I look at Mamãe again. Mamãe smiles and says something. She speaks slowly and sounds a little forced. Rivia explains that she says she used to have a big beauty mark there and had it removed. I smile. Now I know what was missing. Mamãe is wearing a colorful dress that goes to her knees and over that a pink cardigan. She's pretty. She looks happy. I chose a pair of black shorts and an orange top. The dresses I packed just for this moment are still sitting in my trunk of a suitcase. We decide to go into the apartment, and as we all walk up the stairs, I feel an enormous frustration that I don't understand the language. Everything depends on Rivia now. God, how grateful I am to have her here. I think that I must have done something right to have such a wonderful friend.

The door opens, and we step into a nice, bright apartment. On the white wall immediately to our left, the family has put up countless pieces of paper on which they've written various things. I understand a number of them: "Welcome Home," "Joy," "Happiness," and they've made lovely drawings on the slips of paper. I stop by one of them and see that they've drawn the Swedish flag and the Brazilian flag, with the words "Family United" between them. That makes my eyes well up again. It means so much to me that they drew the Swedish flag there and that they see our meeting as uniting. When I look at the two different flags, I see myself: my countries, my different families, my different friends, and my different lives. Mamãe sees my tears and all but apologizes for not crying herself. She says that she's gone through so much in her life that she doesn't cry very easily anymore. I give her the warmest smile I can and say that I really understand and that I can cry for us both. I don't know how much of that Rivia manages to translate before my aunts get going at full speed.

We walk into the little kitchen. I give Mamãe the present I brought for her, a yellow Bon O Bon box, the same kind that I once received from her at the orphanage so many years ago. Mamãe smiles and accepts it. Her eyes start to light up, but I'm not sure it's because she remembers that those are the same chocolates she brought me when I was little. From the mischievous glint in her eyes, I can really tell she has a sweet tooth. My aunt comes running over with a worried look. She says that Mamãe is a diabetic. I nod and say I'd better take the box away from her. When we do that, Mamãe immediately looks displeased. I can't help laughing as I notice that neither she nor I are people who hide our feelings very well. As I smile at Mamãe, I feel a little disappointed that she doesn't seem to remember. Sad that something that came to mean so much to me didn't mean as much to her. Still, there is something moving about the way she takes the box. Mostly I'm disappointed in myself. Here stands the woman who meant so incredibly much to me, and all I brought her was a box of chocolates! What am I, five years old or something? I should have bought her a pretty gold necklace with a locket and a picture of my brother and me. In all seriousness, can you imagine? A box of chocolates that might kill her or make her sick if she ate it! But the box of chocolates really was the most obvious choice for me. I associate it with one of my most wonderful memories from the orphanage. And I wanted to show Mamãe that I remember, that I value everything she did for me, and that I really am her daughter who's come back. Sure, I've changed a lot, but I'm her daughter.

We get a short tour of the apartment, and Mamãe shows me her bedroom. She sits down on the bed and says that she wants me to sleep there with her tonight. It hits me how naturally she suggests that, and I feel so much warmth for her, sitting there on her bed. I wonder if I feel so comfortable with her because of everything we've been through, the history we have together. Or whether it's because I recognize her style so well. She's just like I remember her: gentle, warm, stubborn, nice, funny, loving, and at the same time I can see the temper. I see myself in her in many ways. But I think most of all I feel so comfortable with Mamãe because she's just like I remember her being when she was my security, my love, and my everything.

I smile and say that I have a hotel room but that in the future, when I come visit, we can sleep here together. She looks a little disappointed, but I tell her that there'll be more visits. I don't feel ready yet. After all, so many years have passed, and I need time, time to digest and time to catch up and understand all the emotions that are surfacing.

We walk back to the kitchen where my aunts have laid out an enormous spread. We sit down and eat, and the homemade food is fantastic: chicken, rice, little *empadinhas* with various fillings, vegetables, olives, meat, more meat, and cheese puffs. Of course, we drink Skol, a Brazilian beer, with the food. In the midst of the hum of voices, I think, *Here I am now, sitting here with my mother and my family, but I don't speak Portuguese.* On the spot, I make up my mind to start studying Portuguese as soon as I get home. It's bizarre how a language can just disappear from your head. I glance gratefully at Rivia. What if she weren't here interpreting? It pleases me that my family took such a quick liking to her, and she to them. We eat the good food while chatting about years gone by.

I find out that Mamãe spent another fourteen years living on the street after Patrick and I were adopted. It makes me sad to hear that life was so hard on her for so long. My aunts and my mother are all speaking over one another as they tell the story now. I ask a simple question that requires a yes or no, and I receive a long account of everything conceivable. My friends often tell me that I do this same thing. Rivia says that's the Brazilian way. In all their stories, I try to fish out and understand the things I've wondered about, the details I want to know. My mother left Patrick and me at the children's home, thinking at first, she explains, that it was a school. When Patrick and I were adopted to Sweden, she didn't know where we were, and no one would tell her anything. My aunts hadn't known that Patrick and I were at the children's home, and when they found out and went there to pick us up, they discovered it was an orphanage and that we had been adopted. The orphanage staff told my aunts we weren't there anymore, but no one told them where we'd gone. For the last twenty-four years, no one in my family has known where we were or even if we were still alive. I listen as they talk, and I feel sad. Imagine not knowing where your children are, not knowing whether they're alive.

Vitoria says that Mamãe usually talks to me every night when she goes to bed and that sometimes Vitoria jokes around with her, sticking her head in the door and pretending to be me. She says that she and Mamãe laugh then, and that warms my heart just as much as it pains me to know that she talks to me in the evenings. I want to tell Mamãe that over the years I've talked to her, too, and to tell her about all the times when I've done something or been scared and heard her voice in my head. But I remain quiet. There's too much to take in and navigate, and I hope that we'll have more opportunities in the future to talk to each other properly.

Mamãe says that she used to roam around, searching for Patrick and me. In her attempts to find us, she walked around São Paulo, wandered back to Diamantina, and tried the places where we used to sleep. I ask how long she did that, and the answer hurts me. Vitoria says that my mother has never stopped. They have often found her barefoot, wandering the streets with bloody feet, and when they've picked her up and brought her back, she's disappeared again, back out there searching for us. Vitoria says that from the day my mother moved in with her, one of my cousins would sometimes take my mother out in the car and just drive around for hours so she could search for her children. Mamãe nods and says that she knew I would come back one day. I smile and say of course I would.

What I still don't understand is why no one was told what happened to us. I think the most humane thing the orphanage and the Brazilian courts could have done would have been to let my mother and her family know that we'd been adopted and that we were in Sweden. That would have spared my mother from so much suffering. I picture her wandering the streets with her feet bleeding and feel pain and sorrow.

Vitoria says that she's been my mother's guardian for ten years now. Then I ask her about my mother's illness. Vitoria says that Mamãe is a diabetic and that she needs injections every day. They have to keep a close eye on her diet, and that's not easy because Mamãe has a sweet tooth and is fond of fatty foods. Mamãe interjects that she doesn't like lettuce. I laugh and say that I love lettuce, it's soooo good. Mamãe gives me a playful look as if to say I'm a traitor to the cause, and then shoos me away with her hand. I laugh. It feels so natural to be around her. But now that I've seen her and spent a little time with her, I understand that diabetes isn't the only thing she's suffering from. Vitoria says that Mamãe takes medicine for schizophrenia. A thousand thoughts pop into my head. I try to concentrate. This is tough news to hear, and I do my best to suppress my disappointment. I ask what it's like for Mamãe to live with the disease. Vitoria says that the medicine helps, but that Mamãe sometimes sees people the rest of us can't see. I ask her when the disease began, and Vitoria says that they think it was sometime around when I was born or a few years after that. I quickly try to process what I've heard. I have time to realize that I'm almost the same age Mamãe was when she had me. If I have children, what are the odds that they could inherit this? What if I get sick, too? But most of all, I think about how much of a struggle my childhood was, how I defended my mother, how much I wanted to be with her, and what a shock it was to read confirmation in the paperwork I found as an adult that she was mentally ill. Now they're confirming that this is true, and that she was probably already ill when I was little. I look over at Mamãe and wonder if all those times when I was left on my own had something to do with her illness. I picture us wandering through the wilderness. I'm tired and my feet hurt and they're covered with sores and aching, but Mamãe just keeps walking and tells me to keep up. Even though there are so many good memories, there are a few that I guess I've never really been able to make sense of. *Maybe her illness explains these?* I wonder. I remember Mamãe screaming hysterically for me outside the orphanage, and I wonder if the disease had something to do with that, too. That she did not successfully grasp what she was supposed to do, that she wasn't told anything, that she didn't make it to the court hearing. It's painful to think about this; it brings up feelings of abandonment in me. I know that she never hit us, but she may have left me alone more than she would have needed to if she'd been completely healthy. But most of all, I wonder if on some level I didn't always suspect that the orphanage was right about whether my mother was sick. I can't help but think that maybe I've denied this as an adult because of my strong feelings of loyalty to my mother. I understand that as a child, I didn't know better. But the older I got, it was like I held on even tighter to my denial even though there was a little voice inside me that said otherwise. Even though there were some memories that I couldn't make sense of. I didn't want it to be true, and the only way of holding the doubt at bay was to never even give the slightest credence to that nagging voice that said, *Maybe?* It's hard to admit that I fell victim to the power of denial. Naïve of me, I realize, but at the same time, I see how it also served its purpose. The denial helped me survive. But it hurts when that perfect glass bubble turns out to be cracked. As a child, I wanted to see everything as black or white, and I didn't know any better. Thanks to my pigheadedness, I refused to listen to the little whisper in my head that wondered about Mamãe's mental health as I got older.

Mamãe says God came to her and told her to leave us at the children's home. She says that if she'd known we would be taken away from her, she wouldn't have listened to him. I give her a smile. I have no idea what else to do. I can't just say to her that I'm grateful that "God" told her to do that, because the truth is, I am. I feel cleft in two. In a way, I'm disappointed because I still don't know how much we'll be able to communicate and what her disease really means for us. At the same time,

I'm incredibly impressed that despite her illness, she was able to give me love and warmth and an upbringing and a strong sense of loyalty. I know that these feelings have saved me many times in my life. But most of all, I'm impressed at Little Christiana, who in the middle of all this—in the caves, on the streets, and in the slums—actually survived. For the first time in my life, I realize just what I've survived and how proud I am of that little girl who fought so hard.

Suddenly, Mamãe asks about Patrick again. She's done that several times now. It makes me happy. There's no mistaking her love, which I've always felt.

A lot of things come to light during our conversation. I find out that my biological father's name was Beto and that he was murdered when I was little. I can tell from the way Mamãe talks about him that she really loved him. I try to map out my new-and-old-at-the-same-time family. My mother's mother gave birth to twenty children. "Or, wait now," Vitoria says, and starts debating with her older sister, Elsa, whether there were twenty or twenty-one children. Rivia and I exchange an astonished glance. I ask Rivia to ask my aunts how many cousins I have, and they look at each other in surprise, wave their arms around, and say that they've stopped counting. There goes my idea of trying to look up all my cousins.

Everyone is talking over everyone else, but obviously Mamãe's parents lived in Diamantina. They were pretty comfortable. My maternal grandfather was a generous man. When people needed help, he would loan them money, but he rarely got it back. So little by little, he had loaned out so much that his own family wound up in dire straits. One day when my mother, the youngest of that whole flock of children, was four years old, he took his own life. He shot himself in the head. My grandmother was left on her own with all those children, and she died two years later when my mother was six. Then my mother had to go to Rio de Janeiro, where she lived with her brother. No one really seems to want to tell the whole story. I can tell they don't feel comfortable, but they say that Mamãe's brother had a drinking problem and that he didn't treat my mother well. One day when she was fourteen, she literally jumped out the window to escape. Later, she had her first two children, my older brothers. I ask about them and learn that one is dead, and they don't really know where the other one is. They also say that Mamãe had a son after Patrick and that a wealthy couple who couldn't have children of their own offered her money for him. They offered her money and medical care during her pregnancy and then took the baby. When Mamãe changed her mind and wanted to return the money and get her son back, it was too late. I ask where he is today, but they don't know anything about him. I still remember the scar from the caesarian section that Mamãe showed me during one of her visits to the orphanage when I asked after my new little brother, whom I called Erique. I remember that I wanted to see him, at least once, so I would know what he looked like and know who he was.

After everything I've heard during these hours, I suddenly feel completely wiped out. I can tell that all the interpreting has really taken its toll on Rivia, too. I ask her if maybe we ought to go back to our hotel and rest. She flashes me a look of irritation and says that there's not a chance in the world that she's going to tell my family that we're heading out now when we haven't seen each other in twenty-four years. I know she's right, but I'm so tired. So many things on this trip have made such an impression on me. There've been so many memories to process, and most of all I realize that I was extremely wound up in anticipation of this meeting. I have been for so many years. All those times as a child when I missed Mamãe and wanted to see her, wondered how she was doing and whether she was alive. All those times as a teenager when I thought about her and whispered to her when I was alone. All those

213

times as an adult when I've thought she was probably no longer alive because I couldn't see how she could manage to get herself out of the destitution we'd lived in. All those times I'd wondered what I would say or do when I saw her again, *if* I ever saw her again. And now, so many years later, I'm standing here with this woman I've missed so much, and I'm just completely drained. It's as if I've been carrying the weight of the world on my shoulders. I can finally stop carrying it, but my muscles are cramped and aching. I know I ought to make the most of every single second of this time that life is now giving me with my mother, but all I want to do is go lie down in the bed in the hotel and sleep. I mean, now that we've found each other, I'd really like to believe that we have a new chance and a little more time. But I stay. I have no way of knowing how much time life will give us. And I'm grateful for the time we have now, so I muster up the last little dribble of energy I have left and do my best to enjoy what feels like a miracle.

Eventually we head back to the hotel and rest for a while. Later that evening, there's a party, and I change into a long black-and-white dress. I meet more members of the family, some of my cousins and some of their children. There's loud Brazilian music and laughter and hugging. People are drinking beer, and even though I've never been much of a beer drinker, I'm on my third. Delza, one of my cousins, passes me another beer. I take it and thank her. She laughs, seems pleased with me, and says it's in my blood. The whole family agrees, and I'm proud that they seem to think they can see a bit of the Brazilian in me. Even if it is only in my beer drinking. At the moment, I'm just so happy that I'm welcome here and get to be part of the family. As the evening goes on, a couple of people cautiously wonder whether I'm angry with the family, because everything turned out the way it did. Whether I'm angry because they didn't take care of Mamãe and me when we were living in the cave and on the streets. Whether I'm angry that they gave up and never searched for me and my brother. That they didn't take better care of my mother.

That is hard to answer. I can honestly say that there are still things I wonder about. But I do also understand that we live in such different realities, that life is hard, and that I can't expect to understand everything. What I feel most strongly is that I am so fervently grateful that I got to see them again. I do my very best to convince them that I don't carry any grudge, just joy at being reunited and getting to know them all. After all, bygones are bygones. What could have been done better, who did or didn't do what, what does that matter now? What would be the point of being angry at my family? The future will be what we make it, and I'm not planning to wreck the chance for me and my Brazilian family to find our way back to each other. We hug and start dancing in the little TV room. They teach me some dance steps. Mamãe and I dance with each other. Her hips aren't so good, so we sway from side to side to the beat of the music. Then a faster song comes on, and my aunt Elsa, who's eighty-six, starts full-on dancing, and I don't understand how she can move so smoothly. I can barely keep up. I laugh and think that her genes bode well.

Everyone is taking pictures. We keep dancing, and I can't think of a better, or more Brazilian, way to wrap up the evening. I glance at Mamãe and suddenly realize in my euphoria that it doesn't make any difference to me, to my memories, and to my feelings that she's sick. Given everything she has had to endure and being sick on top of that, she's even stronger than I'd thought to begin with.

When she asks about Patrick again, I tell her that he's coming in a few days and that he's really looking forward to seeing her. I so desperately hope that they'll have a good reunion. Patrick was so little when he and Mamãe were separated, I don't know what kind of relationship they'll build in the future. But I hope they'll have a strong bond, the same way that I hope that my mother and I will keep our strong bond and be close. And at the moment, I have no doubt that will happen.

I've learned that a person can be stripped of everything, but also that everything is possible as long as you never stop walking. And one of the women in my life who taught me this is now standing before me and talking to me as if no time has passed. I call her Mamãe, and my fear that that might feel strange is completely gone.

When I get back to the hotel that night, I search online for information about Mamãe's disease. I don't know very much about schizophrenia. All I know is that it's some form of psychosis that makes a person interpret reality differently from how the rest of us do. And that it's a disease people usually have their whole lives. I read that it develops from a combination of hereditary and environmental factors. There's a genetic susceptibility that makes it more likely that you'll experience psychosis when you're exposed to stressors or difficult experiences. That's the least you could say of what Mamãe has had to go through. I wonder who wouldn't be insane if they were forced to fight every day and on so many different levels to survive.

I spend the following days socializing intensely with my mother and my family. At one point, she asks me whether *I* can see my father or God or Jesus. When I respond that I can't, she seems a little disappointed but says that maybe I will be able to see them one day. I think to myself that I really hope that I won't. I wonder about the times when Mamãe and I sat in our little cave looking out at the beauty of Diamantina—whether the stories that she told me about God and Jesus were times when she was receiving a visit from another world. I've been a little afraid of this moment, that it would feel weird to hear my own mother disappear into another world, or more like another world coming to visit her. To hear her talking to someone the rest of us can't see or hear. But I discover that it feels fine, like a fairy tale from when I was little. Mamãe says that she sees my father—Beto—and God and Jesus. She seems happy when they come to visit, and for some reason it makes me happy, too. She laughs a lot, and I am astounded that after all she's been through, she can still genuinely smile and laugh. I think about what she told me the first day we saw each other again after twenty-four years. How after everything she's been through, she doesn't cry easily anymore. It pains my heart, and I picture the blows that I saw her take when I was a child. She was poorly treated, and I feel my eyes begin to burn. My mother didn't just make sure to give me the words and the strength to keep walking; she never stopped following her own advice. She never stopped walking. And I'm grateful that we have both continued and not given up along the way, and that we have finally walked so far that we've come all the way back to each other.

One night, when we're late getting home, I crawl under the covers and think about Mamãe. I'm sad that she's sick, that no one took care of her or helped her when she was having trouble. Sad that the social-welfare protections that exist in Sweden and other countries don't exist in Brazil. But when I start crying, it's out of pure gratitude. To think that three little words can make such a big difference. Never stop walking. I also think about my other mother, Lili-ann, and how much I wish she were here, sharing this with me. I'm sure that both my mothers would have liked and respected each other. And somewhere in my imagination, I can see Lili-ann, Petronilia, and me in the little cave. My Swedish mother Lili-ann in her fancy clothes, Mamãe Petronilia weaving palm fronds and how they're both yelling at me in unison to be careful and not fall when I climb.

Learning to Breathe Again
1999

After my adoptive mother's passing, I did everything possible not to
feel. All my energy went into not feeling. I had so many emotions, so
many old, new, and especially frightening feelings. So much was totally
different, and yet nothing was new. I was constantly drained and empty.

Not long after my Swedish mother Lili-ann's funeral, I was sitting
alone in my room in our basement in Vindeln. I was staring out at the
darkness. It was night. It was after midnight, and I couldn't sleep. It felt
like there was a weight pushing on me, and every breath was a struggle.
Then quite suddenly, a calm came over me. I could feel the warmth
from the darkness and the security it provided. I felt numb.

I began to try to gain control of myself and my pain. When no one
was looking, I would sit in a corner and try to remember what it felt like
to breathe, to breathe normally. It was hard for me to remember what
you did when you breathed. I would lock myself in one of the school's
restroom stalls and try to find a way to breathe that wasn't like gasping
for air through a straw. Sometimes I looked at myself in the mirror and
thought, at first silently to myself, that everything was going to be OK.
I could fix this. Then I kept looking at the mirror and thought a little
louder: *I will fix this.* Then I opened the restroom door, stepped out into

the school hallway, and smiled at the first person I saw or knew, a smile that said that everything was fine. I rarely asked for help.

Of course, that wasn't enough. Gradually I realized that. Without help, I was going to drown, and once I drowned, there wouldn't be any help. They could do CPR on me for however long they wanted, but the day I drowned, I was going to die. The realization that what comes between breathing and drowning is a little beverage straw was unbelievably frightening. Being aware that everything is falling apart and going to hell is not always best for the feelings of panic. I started to understand the power emotions could have and how hard it can be to change them via rational thought. Pain, grief, rage, hatred, confusion, frustration, bitterness, loss, loneliness, guilt, disappointment, fear, and obligation can all lead to chaos if your emotions are given too much space and have a chance to join forces.

We're all alike and yet so different. If we're subjected to the smallest extra amount of pain, pain that then joins forces with guilt, and then together they find their way home to loneliness, we will find ourselves putting up the strongest of walls. Walls that reason can never penetrate. Reason basically does what it's good at: it works its way around, over, and under the walls.

My foundations were laid when I was little, in the slums and on the streets of Brazil. My foundations were fear, loss, loneliness, physical and mental pain, death, injustice, and a lot of other negative stuff. Thanks to my adoptive mother's stubbornness, love, and desire to do good, I got another chance. Now she was no longer here. For the majority of my life, I had been afraid, afraid of all kinds of different things—a consequence of the unstable foundation that had been laid for me. I was forced to build a wall around myself. And my reason has run around and around it, trying to get in.

On Top of It All
DIAMANTINA, 2015

We're back in the caves, Mamãe, Rivia, and I. The landmark I always looked for when I was little and got lost is there. I sit atop the cave and dangle my legs over the edge. I look at the landmark: a steep, sixty-five-foot-tall white rock. I turn my head and look straight ahead. I am met by a familiar view, Diamantina's wilderness of green mountains stretching as far as the eye can see and the sky, which is clear blue with fluffy cotton-candy clouds. Below me in the cave, I hear Rivia and Mamãe chatting with each other. I inhale the warm air, which is clean, unlike in São Paulo. I hear the crickets. It sounds like I'm surrounded by thousands and thousands of crickets who've decided to play a staccato symphony. I wasn't prepared for the caves to feel so small. Everything's the same, but I feel like a giant sitting here. Mamãe and I used to sit here, and she would tell me her stories.

I listen to Mamãe and Rivia. Mamãe's words come slowly, as if each breath is difficult. Her voice trembles a little, and I can tell from how Rivia is talking to Mamãe that she's gone off into her own world, or that her world has come to visit her here in ours. I hear Mamãe say my father's name, Beto. I have no memory of Beto, my biological father. I try to feel some emotion for this person whose DNA I share, but that's all he and I are ever going to have in common. How can you miss someone you don't remember? My only memory of him is his not being there. I was never mad or upset at him for it. It's hard to be mad or upset at someone you don't know. Since Mamãe said that he'd been murdered, I'm glad I've never been mad at him. It wouldn't be fair to him to be mad at him for not being there when it was physically impossible. Being murdered seems like a valid reason for being absent. But I'm not even curious about who he was. I haven't asked Mamãe about him, and what I know is what she's volunteered to share. Maybe that will change, but right now, all the information, all the questions and ideas I already have about everything else are enough.

My grandmother gave birth to twenty or twenty-one children. My grandfather took his own life. My mother jumped out a window to escape from her brother. My father was murdered. One of my brothers is dead, and no one knows where the other one is, and above all—my mother has schizophrenia. I've got all I can deal with right now just trying to process all this.

I dangle my legs, behold the beauty of Diamantina, and take a deep breath. I try meditating. I want to be able to take in all the beauty before me and bring it home with me to Sweden. I can't meditate. Over the years, I've tried various methods of finding the way to that peaceful silence within. How people manage to do that is a mystery to me. My brain is always in overdrive. I've tried yoga, too. But when I sit there in those various positions and try to forget the world around me, it's like I become hyper-aware of the world around me. But here I sit now, out in this natural setting, looking out at all this beauty, and I think that maybe I can pull it off now.

Wait now . . . Is that a mosquito on my hand? I mean, I have been vaccinated against everything imaginable. I did it at the last minute. The doctor said it wasn't optimal to have the shots so close to leaving on my trip, but that it should work. I feel mosquitoes start sucking my blood, and I wonder what a malaria mosquito looks like. I try to wave the mosquito away, but there are just more and more of them. I have no memory of there being swarms of mosquitoes in the caves when I was little. I realize that there's not going to be any meditating today, either. I'll be happy if I can just get down off this mountain with half my blood left. I yell down to Rivia that I don't recall there being so many mosquitoes. I hear Mamãe laugh a little. Rivia tells me my mother says we used to make smudge fires and burn plants around the cave to keep the mosquitoes away. I yell back that I'm going to climb the white rock behind me to get a better view. Mamãe immediately starts to protest. I can't help but laugh; it's just like when I was little. I climbed, and Mamãe protested. I tell Rivia to assure Mamãe that there's no danger. I kind of know what I'm doing.

On my way toward the cliff face, I realize that the vegetation is out of control. I would need a machete to make any kind of headway through this. Instead, I use my hands and feet to try to create a path. I hear rustling noises in the undergrowth and the small palm trees. I try to summon up the tough little girl inside me, the girl who ran around here as a kid and knew how you made your way through a forest. I'm not looking where I'm going and miss the gigantic spiderweb right in front of my face. I walk straight through it and feel panic rise in me. I run the last little way as hard as I can. The shrubs and branches hit my body, and they burn exactly the way they did that night so many years ago when Mamãe and I ran and hid here.

When I make it to the white cliff face, I leap up onto a big stone. "Ha-ha!" I yell in victory to the plants I just emerged from. I look up toward the top and start climbing. I have always loved using my body. It feels right. We're not supposed to sit around all day long in an office in front of a computer. We're supposed to use our bodies to run, climb, jump, dance. I very quickly realize that sneakers are not ideal. I miss my climbing shoes, which I left in my closet back home in Umeå. I hear Rivia calling to me from where she and my mother stand waiting until they can see me on the top of the rock. "How's it going?"

"It's a little harder to climb than I remember, but it's going fine," I yell back.

Finally, I reach the top. From here, I can see the countryside spread out around me. I know that there are lots of beautiful places on earth, but at the moment, I can't think of any that can touch the wilderness around Diamantina, the clear blue of the sky meeting the green of the forest. Even if I'm no longer a cave girl, I'm happy that I feel such a strong sense of kinship with this place. An overwhelming sense of joy and peace fills me. This is a part of me, and I am a part of this. I laugh and wave to Mamãe and Rivia. I yell down to them how extraordinarily beautiful it is up here, and Rivia responds that Mamãe says I should be careful.

If I've ever doubted where I got my stubbornness from, I won't need to do so anymore, because during these days I've seen the same pigheadedness in my mother that I see in myself. I'm up on the top, and she's standing down below me, yelling. It's nice—funny, but nice—to have a mother again and as an adult woman to hear what to do and not do. *I can get used to this,* I think, and untie the Brazilian flag that I've had around my waist.

I spread my feet on top of the cliff, grab the ends of the flag, and let the wind catch the fabric. I feel the flag fluttering and tugging behind me. I scream at the top of my lungs. I laugh, and I scream again. It feels good. Finally, I'm standing on a mountain peak and screaming at the top of my lungs. It occurs to me that maybe I've never been able to really scream before because I haven't been on top of the right mountain.

As I stand here, looking back on everything that's happened to me, I can see the beauty in it. I can see the good in it despite everything I've had to fight for. It has hurt, it has been hard, but of course there have been wonderful moments, filled with joy and love. I can suddenly see something beautiful in the dark times. It probably would have been different if I'd been standing here on this mountain with only Rivia looking up at me. But my mother is here now, and it feels like we've come full circle. I found the woman who in eight years gave me enough love, courage, and strength to keep me walking forward through my life. It will have to do.

Life sees to it that we lose everything, and one day I will lose my biological mother again, but the memories I will take with me are most of all the uplifting memories of how she helped me buck up, again and again. I stand here as a grown-up on top of my mountain and look at her, seeing her problems with one of her hips and knowing she needs to take insulin for diabetes and pills for schizophrenia. Still, when she talks to me with her calmness, and even though God and Jesus and my dead father come to visit her, wisdom and love are there nevertheless. Right now, I wouldn't want to change any part of my life, because that would mean changing other parts, parts that have caused me to grow and made me into who I am today.

I wave again to Mamãe and Rivia, and laugh. I decide to scream one more time.

Back to Northern Sweden
2015

I'm standing at the baggage claim at the airport in Umeå, Sweden, waiting for my trunk of a suitcase to show up. I flew the last leg, from Stockholm to Umeå, by myself. Rivia is heading off to two weddings. How she can be up for that after the trip we've just been on is a mystery to me. But I suppose she's a true Amazon, and I guess they can handle just about anything. I see my bag, and I struggle to lift it off the baggage carousel. I tip it up onto its little wheels and pull it toward the exit. Even though it's about nine o'clock at night, it isn't dark yet. I walk out of the terminal and search for a familiar metallic-blue Volvo. Fredrik, a skydiving friend, offered to pick me up. I didn't know whether I'd be lonely when I came back from my trip, and now that I see him, I'm glad I texted him from the airport in Stockholm and asked him to come. I climb into the car. Fredrik closes the trunk and gets in behind the wheel, starts the car, and drives out of the airport, heading toward my apartment. He asks how my trip was, and I give him a look of exhaustion. "We'll talk about it after we get you home," he says, and I nod. While he drives, I look at him. There was a time when I was in love with this man and he with me. We made a mess of that, but we've managed to hold on to the friendship.

Once we're up in my apartment, we sit on my gray sofa, and he puts his arm around me. During my trip, there wasn't time to stop and process my thoughts and emotions. It's going to take a long time for me to sift through all the new information, all the new thoughts and feelings that have come up but also through the old ones that have always been there. But I get out my computer and show him all the pictures from the trip. I try to explain what happened, answer all his questions, and we laugh and cry together. I'm glad to be sharing this with a friend who knows me well. I wouldn't have wanted to be alone this evening.

We sleep, and when I wake up in the morning, I say goodbye to Fredrik and sit back down on my sofa. Suddenly everything is so peaceful. I have no appointments to keep, nowhere I need to be, no new place I need to see, no new people I need to meet. I look around my apartment and note that it is light, airy, fresh, and clean. Wonderful! So, now what, Christina? It's completely quiet, eerily quiet. Where is all the noise—traffic noise, construction noise, people talking, cars honking, loud music? Has Umeå always been this quiet? Has Umeå always been this lonely? A familiar panic begins to creep over me. Everything feels so strange. I'm home, I feel like I'm home, but now I have another home. I take a deep breath, and my whole body starts itching as I sit there on my sofa.

I pick up the phone and call Maja. Maja already welcomed me home. I talked to her on the phone when I landed in Stockholm. She's home in Röbäck with the kids, Harry and my little goddaughter, Greta. She's making lunch and wonders if I want to come over. I jump into my shoes, lunge for my car keys, and jog down the stairs and out the door.

Ten minutes later, I take the E4 across the beautiful Ume River, which glitters where the sunlight hits the surface. Once I reach Maja's house, I turn off the engine and wander up to her front door. I knock a bit quietly, mostly for show, but I don't wait for anyone to open the front door. Instead, I just walk in. Harry runs to me with his arms out, crying, "Kicki, Kicki, Kicki!" I squat down and exclaim, "Harry, Harry,

Harry!" and Harry runs right into my arms and hugs me. The best love you can get. Then Greta comes. "Titti, Titti, Titti!" Another hug. Maja comes to the door and gives me a big hug. God, how I needed this!

We walk into the kitchen, and I sit down at the kitchen table and start recounting. I could never have imagined how much this trip would affect me. Getting to share this with my friends is my salvation.

By the next day, I've adjusted to the silence a little more, and although I miss Brazil and my family, it's nice to be home again. I decide to bike into the city and go to Åhlén's, the department store, to do something normal and mundane.

I'm looking at some throw pillows when I run into an old high school friend. "Hey, Christina!" she says, and smoothly steps out from behind her stroller to give me a hug. I smile but feel really tired and not up to chatting with anyone, so I hope she doesn't ask too many questions. "That was some trip you took," she says, mentioning that she followed me on Instagram. "Tell me everything," she continues.

I smile a little and say that that would probably take too long. I change the topic. She takes the bait and starts talking about the new house they're building. Evidently a feud has arisen between them and one of the families that will be their new neighbors. She gives me an extremely detailed blow-by-blow description of the drama and finishes by saying that she threatened to file a police report. I feel the small amount of energy I had managed to regain after my trip being sucked right out of me. The person in front of me just keeps talking about some road that was built ten years ago, neighbors, and petty disputes. I cut her short in midsentence and say, "Hey, I've just returned from an orphanage where the kids hardly have a future. The kids there told me about how their parents mistreated them, how adults have abused and exploited them, how they've been separated from the siblings they love, and how they don't know whether they'll ever get to see them again.

One little boy watched his father be murdered. People dumped gasoline on him and set him on fire. So, you know what? I'm not really up to hearing about first-world problems at the moment."

She stares at me, her eyes wide, and I realize that I should have handled this whole thing more tactfully. She says, "Oh my God, how terrible!" and continues. "That's just what I'm trying to say. I sent the lady next door a text where I said just that, that there are children starving on the other side of the world, and that we shouldn't . . . ," and then she gets going again. I interrupt her and say that I have a meeting to get to.

This is one of the things I've had a hard time understanding and getting used to growing up. We live in such different realities. If you've always lived in a safe and secure world, with a house and money, a mother and a father, children and a husband, a social safety net, access to healthcare, without war—the list can get quite long—then it seems to be so hard to understand and see things from the perspective of someone living in a much harder and more dangerous reality.

Back home in my lovely, quiet apartment, I take out a pen and a pad of paper. I write: *What do I want to do with my life?* Beneath that, I write: *Change. Find balance in life. Help other people.*

A bit later, I call Rivia and ask if she can come over so we can Skype Mamãe.

Rivia comes almost right away. She asks if I have the phone number, and I read it to her while she types it into Skype. With mixed emotions, I sit and listen to the ringtone. I wonder if Vitoria or Mamãe will answer, if anyone will answer at all. Vitoria answers, and Rivia explains who she is. She gives me a look of encouragement, and in faltering Portuguese I manage to say, "Hi, Vitoria, it's Christina." Vitoria greets me and keeps on talking. Rivia interprets. Vitoria says everyone is doing well. She wonders when I'll be back to visit, and I respond that I'll come as soon as I have the time and the money. I tell Rivia that I'd like to speak to Mamãe. Rivia asks for Mamãe. I hear Vitoria chatting with Mamãe and explaining that Rivia and I are on the phone. I hear Mamãe's voice, and I smile. I say, "Hi, Mamãe, how are you doing?" in Portuguese, and Rivia smiles at me encouragingly. Mamãe responds, and it's a little hard to make out what she says. Rivia steps in to help. I ask how Mamãe is doing and if she got to see her girlfriend in Diamantina. She's doing well but didn't get to visit with her girlfriend. She tells me that the next time I come down, we'll go to the cave and make ourselves a meal there. I smile and say that I'm really looking forward to it. Mamãe says we can sleep there. I say, "Hmm," but think to myself that maybe I'm not really looking forward to spending the night outdoors with poisonous snakes, spiders, scorpions, and centipedes in the dark—not as much as Mamãe seems to be. Mamãe is happy when I say that we'll visit our cave again, and she quickly says that my last visit was far too short. She keeps chatting, and Rivia looks at me. I can tell from her face that she is complaining about me a little. Instead of translating all of that, Rivia summarizes what she said. "She's disappointed that you didn't stay longer, that you didn't stay for her birthday, that you're not there now. She wonders when you're coming back." I respond that I'll come as soon as I can and have money. Mamãe says that I have four trillion, so I can come when I want. Rivia and I can't help but laugh. The idea that everyone who lives in Sweden is filthy rich has apparently reached my family. I try to explain to Mamãe, but Rivia says there's no point. Obviously, I already know that, but for the sake of my own conscience, I still want to try. I don't want her to feel like I don't want to see her.

I promise Mamãe I'll be back as soon as I have the time and money for it. I promise to stay several weeks the next time I come down, and I promise to call her once a month. After I tell her I love her, miss her, and that we'll talk again soon, we hang up. It's quiet for a few seconds, and then my eyes meet Rivia's. A thousand emotions are rushing through me. Incredible! I just talked to my mother in Brazil. It's magical! We're in touch now. Rivia smiles and says that it's time for me to get to work on my Portuguese.

There's a warmth in my body, but so many thoughts are swirling around in my head. Of course, everything isn't suddenly easy and uncomplicated. I start to realize that for as many problems as the trip solved, just as many new ones have arisen. How am I going to communicate with my mother? I mean, I want to get more out of our contact. How can I provide for her? Are they expecting that of me? Am I expecting that of myself? How can I stay in touch with my family? I mean, my life is here, in Sweden, at least right now. But the most positive of all is that I feel like I've already been changed by my trip and by meeting people and experiencing Brazil. I'm filled with the sensation of having two homes, two worlds—and the two people who are both me can maybe finally be interwoven into one. I don't believe that life is about finding yourself. For me, life is about creating your own reality. And I ask myself this question: Who do I want to be?

A few months later, that question is easier to answer. I have started my own company. I've started doing public speaking, which includes telling people my history, among other things. I want to work on the issues of identity, prejudice, culture clashes, and multicultural issues, and I want to inspire others. I've started a foundation that will work with vulnerable children and teenagers, in Brazil among other places. We have already started collaborating with my orphanage in São Paulo. I want to contribute to something besides helping the world consume more. My meeting with the kids at the orphanage made it clear to me that I have to do this.

I'm so happy and proud to be both Brazilian and Swedish and to represent both cultures. I have felt a sense of guilt and shame my whole life, been so hard on myself, felt like I had to handle everything on my own. But now as I think of who I am today, I'm actually pleased with myself. My God, I'm far from perfect. I have plenty of flaws, and I've done things I regret and things I'm ashamed of. But on the whole, I'm pleased with myself. I'm not just Swedish; I'm also Brazilian, and it feels amazing. I have had and continue to have a good life. I've received more than I could hope for, both good and bad. This has shaped me into a person who, after many years, I can accept and like. I've accepted that what has happened, has happened. The hardest thing has been forgiving myself for what I've done, but also what I've believed I've done. Coming to terms with myself is a long journey, and I feel like I'm on my way.

Afterword

I've heard that a decently long human life lasts for about 650,000 hours. I've spent a little more than 70,000 hours of my life in Brazil's streets and slums, and in the wilderness around Diamantina. If I get to live a long life—a whole 650,000 hours—that will mean that I will have lived more than a tenth of my life destitute, struggling every day to survive.

I cannot say today that I'm angry that I was adopted, but I was and remain upset that I never got to say goodbye to my birth mother, that no one ever explained to me what adoption would entail until it was too late for me to make my own choice. I'm angry that my mother didn't receive any assistance, that she was left on the streets to her fate. I'm furious at a society that chose and continues to choose to just look away or not to look at all. More than two hundred million people live in Brazil today, and I wonder how many million individuals, how many million children, are being raped and beaten and how many are huffing glue to deaden the hunger that kills so many far too soon. How many of them have given up hope, accepted that they're not worth anything, and turned to crime? How many of these people could we save? How many do we want to save?

Where is the morality in a society that lines up innocent children and guns them down in cold blood? What does society expect abused, vulnerable children to grow up and become? Well-adjusted, contributing citizens? These children are growing up with their souls crushed. They will act out based on what they've learned. Why should they make any effort when no one has ever made any effort for them? And yet they give so much of themselves. Trust must be earned, and that seems to be something that Brazil has not understood. Rather than building trust, the country has built walls to separate the rich from the poor.

There are times when I think back, when I relive experiences and recall things that happened, that I'm ashamed to be a human being. How can people allow such things to go on? I feel angry at a country and at a people who just shut their eyes to the suffering around them. But most of all, I'm angry and sad that they choose not to see the value in all human beings, in all the beauty that is there.

It's easy to say things without reflecting. People have told me that I must be strong to have done so well despite the tough life I've had, that I'm surely a better person after all I've been through. I can't say that I'm strong. I can't say that I'm weak, either, no weaker than anyone else. I've just handled the various situations that life has given me as well as I could or dared.

Why should what I've been through make me a better person? Sure, at times I may have a more firsthand understanding of what some people go through in life. But why should my experiences make me a better person? What I've gone through, experienced, and seen has hurt my soul. It's given me baggage that I've been afraid to share with the people I care about, baggage that could have made me hateful. Over the years, I've tried not to go down that path. But shouldn't a child who's gone through what I have, grow up to be hateful and *not* a better person? Would it really be so strange if I were more wicked than good? People sometimes tell me that they could never have made it through what I've been through, but the truth is that millions of people go through similar experiences, and much worse, every day. We humans are amazing creatures! We're built to take significantly more than we think we can. But we're often selfish, and when everything comes to a head, when it's a matter of survival, most people choose to fight at the expense of others. I wish I hadn't had to witness this. I'm neither bad nor good, better nor worse. I'm a human being, just like all the rest who carry this kind of heavy baggage. But I did receive something fundamental that all people need: the knowledge that there's love and that extreme poverty does not prevent love. My biological mother, my brother, Camile, and Patricia taught me that in Brazil. My adoptive mother and father and my good friends in Sweden did, too.

Life is fragile, and humans are vulnerable. We need care and joy. There are so many kindhearted people who prove that there is love, and thus there is hope.

Today, I worry about the changes I see in many of the world's more fortunate countries. In the wonderful country I live in, Sweden, which I have come to love as my own, refugees stream in, and you see panhandlers and street children more and more often. At the same time, people and politicians close their eyes to the new problems that have arisen. They don't have the experience to handle the changes that our country, like so many others, faces. Many of us want to help but don't know how. We might open our borders to these poor people who are fleeing war and misery, but there is no plan of action for how to integrate them into our society. And somewhere along the way, their humanity is forgotten. I sincerely hope that Sweden and the rest of the world find a humane path forward through these crises. We must understand that it does no good to wish for how things were—the past is the past.

Change is painful. It's uncomfortable and sometimes even distressing. But if we embrace the change and look at the positive in it and strive to make the best of it, there's so much good to be gained. Viewing situations as *us* versus *them* is dangerous. No good can come of that mentality. I fervently hope that no army in Sweden or anywhere else will need to be part of what I experienced in Brazil. I don't want to see societies filled with good people changed to such an extent that we close our eyes to a young girl being murdered without punishing the perpetrators. This must never feel normal. I never want us to look at another individual and think we're more valuable because we're richer or have a different skin color, sexual orientation, or religion.

Although I did not receive professional help as a child, I had an adoptive family that cared for me, a school where the teachers and students accepted me, and a society that welcomed me. I was accepted because my Swedish parents were a part of that society, and so I automatically was, too.

It is so profoundly upsetting to me to think of all these refugee children arriving alone, children who have fled from war and extreme poverty in the hope of a new chance in life. It hurts to know that they, who are already carrying so much—the loss of those who were near and dear to them, violence they've had to witness or endure, the loss of faith in humanity and life—are coming to a country that will not wholeheartedly include them in its society. I can honestly tell you that I don't think I could have handled coming to a new country and not feeling welcome. I wish we could all stop for a second and ask ourselves: What are we doing for these children and these people? What can we do? How would we want to be treated if this happened to us? What difficulties do you encounter when you come to a new land? Let us join together and see the human being, see ourselves in these human beings who need help.

To survive, I was forced to adapt to what was expected of me. But in doing so, I was also forced to give up a part of myself. Although there was so much goodwill, over the years I've amassed feelings that

I have hidden or locked away. I split my soul in two. Sometimes I've flourished that way; sometimes I have not. But most of all, I've tried to understand and tried to forgive—to forgive the past, what I've done and what others have done to me. I have so many regrets that make me sad—that I never said, "I love you" or "Goodbye" to my second mother, Lili-ann, for example. Rarely do we regret something we've said to those we love. What we usually regret are the things we never said. I've been afraid to love and afraid of not being loved for who I am. But on some level, I've always held out hope that in the future I would be strong enough to be able to work through everything and become whole again. That involves extensive work in coming to terms with the little girl who was scared for most of her childhood, adrift as a teenager, and cleft in two as an adult.

As I read what I've written, I note that the process of writing has done just what I wished: helped me along my path. It's nice to have finished my book project. It hasn't been easy confronting so many difficult memories. It's been painful but also gratifying work. Sometimes it feels like I'm reading about someone else's life. It feels impossible that I could have gone through all this. The two worlds are so different, living on the streets in Brazil and not knowing whether I'd have food to eat that day, and then coming to a country where people throw food away on a daily basis. There's no logic to it. It feels like I'm reading about a former life, and if it weren't for my having such strong emotions and dreams about what's happened, if it weren't for it having hurt so much and left such deep marks, I would believe I was reading someone else's story.

What I didn't understand while I was growing up in Sweden was that I was experiencing massive culture shock. What's Swedish? What's Brazilian? Who am I? The experience is hard to describe. That, too, has left deep marks on me. Yes, these marks were made during a winding journey between two parts of the world, and a path like this is never simple or ready-made. At every crossroads, courage is required to decide which way to go. You need to dare to step out into the unknown, and you must be prepared for it to turn your life upside down.

Today I am happy and proud of my life. And this isn't the end of my story. It's just the beginning. I carry my mother's words with me: *Always keep walking. Never stop walking.*

ACKNOWLEDGMENTS

My profoundest thanks to:

Petronilia Maria Coelho and Lili-ann Rickardsson: Everything good in me comes from you.

Patrick Rickardsson: I love you. Nothing more needs to be said.

My childhood friends: Camile, Patricia, Santos, Maja (Fahlgren) Lindberg, Emma Allebo, Lina Nordlund, Anna-Karin Lundström. You're more than friends. You're my family.

Rose-Inger Danielsson: What a wonderful aunt and human being you are! Thank you for always knowing what's up with me.

Thank you to my newfound family in Brazil.

And thank you to my father, Sture Rickardsson.

Others I'd like to thank: Rivia Oliveira, Anna Stenbäck, Nils Lundmark, Patrick Krainer, Pontus Berg, Pernilla Holmberg, Siri Olsson, Stefan Holm, Inga-Britt von Essen, Federico Luna, Malin Söderström.

I could never have dreamed I would have such wonderful friends and that you would stand by me through this life. I am so grateful. Without you, I think I would have floundered. I appreciate all the times you've listened, given advice, scolded me, and loved me. I don't have the words to describe what you've meant and continue to mean to me. The words that I can find now are "I love you."

To all my skydiving friends: You know who you are, and you're all amazing. You invited me into a world of so much love and warmth. I hope that I give you just as much joy as you have given and continue to give me. *Thank you!* The sky is not the limit; the ground is!

A big thanks to all the teachers and the rest of you who have ever been there for me. You will probably never know what a difference you've made and how much you mean to me.

A big thanks to my English-language publisher, AmazonCrossing.

And a big thanks to my Swedish publisher, Teresa Knochenhauer, to my editor Liselott Wennborg Ramberg, and to everyone at Bokförlaget Forum.

Christina & Christiana

ABOUT THE AUTHOR

Photo © 2016 Helén Karlsson

Christina Rickardsson was born in 1983 as Christiana Mara Coelho in Brazil. At the age of seven, she was taken to an orphanage along with her younger brother and then out to Vindeln, a village located in the north of Sweden in a region called Västerbotten. After Christina finished her memoir, *Never Stop Walking*, she founded the Coelho Growth Foundation, which brings awareness to the plight of child poverty.

ABOUT THE TRANSLATOR

Photo © 2006 Libby Lewis

Tara Chace has translated more than twenty-five novels from Norwegian, Swedish, and Danish. Her most recent translations include Bobbie Peers's *William Wenton and the Impossible Puzzle* (Simon & Schuster, 2017), Martin Jensen's The King's Hounds trilogy (AmazonCrossing, 2013–2015), Sven Nordqvist's Pettson and Findus books (NorthSouth, 2014–2016), and Jo Nesbø's Doctor Proctor's Fart Powder series (Aladdin, 2010–2014).

An avid reader and language learner, Chace earned her PhD in Scandinavian languages and literature from the University of Washington in 2003. She enjoys translating books for adults and children. She lives in Seattle with her family and their black lab, Zephyr.